PANCHAYATI RAJ

THE ROLE OF PANCHAYATS IN INTEGRATED RURAL DEVELOPMENT

PANCHAYATI RAJ

THE ROLE OF PANCHAYATS IN INTEGRATED RURAL DEVELOPMENT

B.L. SHAH
Department of Political Science
Kumaun University
Nainital

COSMO PUBLICATIONS
NEW DELHI INDIA
1990

Made in India
First Published 1990

PANCHAYATI RAJ
The Role of Panchayats in Integrated Rural Development

Published by:
RANI KAPOOR (MRS.)
COSMO PUBLICATIONS
for Genesis Publishing (P) Ltd.
24-B-Ansari Road, Darya Ganj,
New Delhi - 110002.
India

Lasertypeset by:
PRINTMAKERS, New Delhi - 110065.

Printed at :
MEHRA OFFSET PRESS
1979, Chandni Mahal
DELHI-110006
Phone No. 268574

PREFACE

The programme of rural development in India is of prime importance because India is predominantly rural having nearly 80 per cent population residing in villages. Economically also, the rural masses are too backward. Great stress was laid during the freedom movement for rural development in all spheres—social, economic, cultural, political, etc. Mahatma Gandhi, 'Father of the Nation', was particularly emphatic about Gram Swaraj which meant an all round development of the villages. The Indian Science Congress at its Waltair session in 1976 took up the theme 'Science and Integrated Rural Development'. Since then, the idea has caught on and at present several districts have been selected for Integrated Rural Development.

Immediately after Independence, the Government of U.P. took steps to organize village panchayats all over U.P. through U.P. Panchayati Raj Act (1947). The aim was to extend local self-government to the grassroots. These panchayats were expected to carry on various schemes of rural development in the countryside. During the second half of the present century, a great revolution in the direction of rural development took place all over India with the introduction of schemes for community development. The pioneer work in this direction was the celebrated report of Balwantrai Mehta Committee 1957. In response to its recommendations, a three tier structure of rural local self-governing bodies with village panchayats at the bottom, development blocks in the middle and the Zila Parishad at the apex was established. The development blocks were to be the centres of all-sided development in the countryside. In this set-up, the panchayats being the grassroot organizations have a great role to play in making the scheme of Integrated Rural Development a success.

Although vast sums of money are spent through the development blocks on different developmental projects, yet the achievements of these projects have not been assessed and are not upto the mark. The main problem is the degree of people's participation desired which is conspicuously lacking.

Kumaun Division comprising the hill districts of Almora, Nainital and Pithoragarh has peculiar geographical and economic features. The vast population of this area resides in small habitations known as villages. They are economically very backward and the topographical conditions prevailing in these hill districts need special attention for rural development. With the inauguration of the three-tier structure of rural local self-government and community development in the countryside, wherein the village panchayats are to serve as basic instruments of Integrated Rural Development, a thorough and specialized study of the role of village panchayats in integrated rural development programme in this backward hill region of Kumaun has been attempted in this work.

The rural development schemes at the micro level of the district are at present formulated by the officers of the Government Departments such as Irrigation, Agriculture, Roads and Buildings, Electricity, Education, Health, etc. based on their normal annual funds. The District Development Plans now being prepared are generally a compilation of the shemes of individual departments without any long term perspective for development and without adequate comprehension of the interaction between physical and socio-economic variables. The implementation of the schemes also suffers from lack of co-ordination and proper fixation of priorities.

The result of such planning is that when an irrigation project is ready, there may not be developed agricultural land to utilize the water and the power line might be running in a different direction. When agriculture produce is ready, there may not be marketing centres and warehousing facilities, nor transport feeder network for marketing centres. The land-colonization centres might not be connected to the transport network and the education and health facilities might be missing due to lack of co-ordinated approach.

Hence, there is urgent need to involve the various specialists and the people themselves in this gigantic task of total integrated approach for mobilization of rural energy to strengthen the agro-industrial base of Kumaun hills and to exploit the natural resources in harmony with environment.

ACKNOWLEDGEMENTS

An intellectual debt is too complex an entity to acknowledge in a brief space. My comments here are to express gratitude for immediate and direct assistance in the production of this book. The research which produced this work would have been impossible without the valuable guidance of my worthy guide, Dr. G.D. Tewari, Assistant Director of Higher Education (Retd.), Allahabad. I am also indebted to, Dr. S.L. Shah, Professor and Head, Agricultural Economics Department, Pantnagar University, whose great qualities of scholarship, initiatives, perseverance and hard labour have always inspired me to advance and grow.

I am also indebted to the many officials who patiently answered my questions. Likewise, I was helped by farmers, rural people and official assistance everywhere I went, my appreciation to all of them is great.

This book is sincerely written in the spirit of inquiry, though it may not always read that way; it should be taken as an investigation, not a pronouncement, and considered a beginning, not an end.

CONTENTS

LIST OF TABLES

LIST OF ABBREVIATIONS

I.R.D.	-	Integrated Rural Development
V.L.W.	-	Village Level Worker
B.D.O.	-	Block Development Officer
P.R.	-	Panchayati Raj
M.L.A.	-	Member of Legislative Assembly
M.P.	-	Member of Parliament
C.D.	-	Community Development
C.O.P.P.	-	Report of the Team for the Study of Community Projects and National Extension Service
A.D.O.	-	Assistant Development Officer
P.W.D.	-	Public Works Department
D.F.O.	-	District Forest Officer
H.Y.V.	-	High Yielding Variety
D.M.	-	District Magistrate
S.F.D.A.	-	Small and Marginal Farmer's Development Agency
D.P.A.P.	-	Drought Prone Area Programme
C.A.D.P.	-	Command Area Development Project
M.F.A.L.	-	Marginal Farmers and Agricultural Labourers Development Agency
N.E.S.	-	National Extension Service
N.A.	-	Not Available
K.S.	-	Kshettra Samitis
Z.P.	-	Zila Parishads
S.C.	-	Scheduled Caste

1
INTRODUCTION

The Idea and Concept of Integrated Rural Development

One has to make a choice between India of the villages which are as ancient as the land herself and India of the cities which are the creation of modern age. Today the cities dominate and drain the villages so that the latter are crumbling to ruin. Gandhiji once observed, "My khadi mentality tells me that cities must subserve villages when that domination goes. Exploiting of villages is itself organised violence. If we want Swaraj to be built on non-violence we will have to give the villages their proper place."[1] The villages are the oldest units of community life known to India and have survived through centuries. The foundation of any democratic structure in India must, therefore, be in the village.

There was virtual stagnation in Indian rural economy during the British rule. After 1858, the British rulers began to think seriously about the desirability of creating institutions of local self-government in India. There was, however, progressive, though slow and gradual development in this direction. It was only by about 1920, that the first serious steps were taken to establish Village Panchayats in selected villages.

The post-Independence period witnessed momentous developments in the field of rural local self-government. Several influences were at work in making the leaders of free India take interest in the revival and reconstruction of village panchayats. Adoption of the Panchayati Raj schemes in the Indian countryside was the outcome of the enormous influence that Gandhiji's philosophy exercises on those who were at the helm of affairs in the years following Independence. Mahatma Gandhi, 'Father of the Nation', was particularly emphatic about Gram Swaraj which meant an all round development of the villages.

Free India's Constitution provides a directive: "The State shall take steps to organise village panchayats and endow them with such powers and authority as may be necessary to enable them to function as units of self-government."[2] The directive was followed broadly by the State Governments and this resulted not only in providing for a net work of the village panchayats all over the country, but also for strengthening rural local self-government by replacing the old District

1. Gandhi, M.K., Rebuilding Our Villages, p.3
2. Article 40

Boards which had practically lost all vitality as such with a three-tier-structure of democratic decentralization having Village Panchayats at the bottom, the Panchayat Samitis in the middle and the Zila Parishad at the apex. Another factor which influenced the development of rural local government was the Community Development Movement inaugurated on October 2, 1952. Thus, rural local self-government has been completely reorganized in the post-Independence period. Since 1957, almost all the States have reorganized their system of rural local self-government mainly on the lines recommended by the Balwantrai Mehta Committee.[3]

Immediately after Independence, the Government of U.P. took lead in passing legislation on Panchayati Raj in 1947.[4] The aim was to extend local self-government to the grassroots. The village panchayats were expected to carry on various schemes of rural development in the countryside besides functioning as basic units of rural local self-government.

In response to the recommendations of Balwantrai Mehta Committee (1957), a three tier-structure of rural local self-government bodies in each district with Village Panchayats at the bottom, Kshettra Samitis in the middle and Zila Parishad at the apex, was established through the U.P. Kshettra Samitis and Zila Parishad Adhiniyam 1961.[5] The then existing N.E.S. Development Blocks were to be the centre of all sided development in the countryside. In this set-up, the panchayats being the grossroot organizations were expected to play a vital role in the community development programme.

Integrated Rural Development became the central theme of rural development since the year 1976. The Indian Science Congress in its Waltair Session held in January 1976, took up the theme "Science and Integrated Rural Development." The basic idea is to undertake intensive development in 2000 out of 3000 blocks already covered under any of the three special programmes of SFDA, DPAP and CADP. Three hundred additional blocks are being brought under the programme during each year of the medium-term plan. Thus, by the end of the Sixth Plan, 3500 blocks would stand covered under the I.R.D.

The policies and programmes of the present government have given importance to changing the faces of the so long neglected villages. This programme has given a chance to the leaders at the local level to help the people to take the opportunities offered by the plan to change their socio-economic condition.. With the establishment of Gaon Panchayats direct democracy has not percolated even in the countryside. The members of these panchayats are expected to give the lead by selfless service to the people by organizing them to participate actively to achieve better results than in the past.

3. Committee on Plan Project (C.O.P.P.) appointed by the Govt. of India in 1957 under the chairmanship of Balwantrai Mehta.
4. UP. Panchayati Raj Act 1947, came into force on 15th August, 1949.
5. U.P. Act XXXIII of 1961.

In 1978, the Union Government set up a Committee with Sri Ashoka Mehta as Chairman, to review the working of Panchayati Raj institutions and in particular, among other things, to suggest their role in the task of integrated rural development. The terms of reference of the Ashoka Mehta Committee required it to suggest measures for reorganizing the Panchayati Raj system and its institutions to play an effective role in the sphere of Integrated Rural Development. The terms of reference were in brief to review the existing situation regarding democratic decentralization in the States and the Union Territories, and the working of the Panchayati Raj institutions from the district to the village levels, so as to identify shortcomings and defects; to examine, in particular, the working of these institutions in respect of mobilization of resources; looking after the interest of the weaker sections of society; methods of constituting the Panchayati Raj institutions, including the system of elections suggesting the role of Panchayati Raj institutions for I.R.D; recommending the relationship that should exist between the Panchayati Raj institutions, the official administrative machinery, and the cooperative and voluntary institutions involved in rural development; and to make such other recommendations, including those on financial matters as may be necessary to ensure adequate availability of funds for the discharge of the responsibilities that may be entrusted to the Panchayati Raj institutions.[6]

The Ashoka Mehta Committee submitted its report in August 1978 making 132 recommendations to revitalize Panchayati Raj as a living and integral part of the democratic continuum. The most significant recommendation of the Committee is for the creation of a two tier system of Panchayati Raj,[7] as against the three tier system recommended by C.O.P.P. and enforced so far. As regards taxation, the Ashoka Mehta Committee wants the Panchayati Raj institutions to have 'compulsory powers of taxation'[8] to mobilise necessary resources on their own thereby reducing their dependence on devolution of funds from the State government. A remarkable feature of the Mehta Report is its recommendation favouring 'open participation'[9] of political parties in Panchayati Raj affairs. The Committee has also made some very interesting recommendations favouring the creation of certain monitoring forums to safeguard and promote the interests of the vulnerable social and economic groups in the villages.[10] An important recommendation of the Committee is that the State government must not supersede the Panchayati Raj institutions on partisan grounds. If, however, the supersession of a body becomes necessary,

6. Cf. Terms of reference; Report of the Committee on Panchayati Raj Institutions, New Delhi, Ministry of Agriculture and Irrigation, Govt. of India, Aug. 1978, p. iv.
7. Ibid, para IV. 6, IV 6.1, IV. 6.2
8. Ibid, para IX. 12.2, IX. 5.4
9. Ibid, para IV, 14.
10. Ibid, para VII, 11.1.

there should be an election within six months.[11] The principal thesis of the Ashoka Mehta Report is the functional necessity for the decentralization of administration and a truly democratic supervision over the latter.

It is now felt that planning should be resource-oriented and science and technology should be brought to bear on the development of resources like animals, land, plant, water, minerals, etc. and their utilization should be optimised over time. India has vast human resources, but much of this resource is unemployed or under-employed. Strategies have to be devised so that every person is enabled to engage himself in a productive and socially useful occupation and earn an income that would meet at least his basic minimum needs.

During the first three plant periods, economic development of several backward regions, particularly the hill districts did not receive much attention except for some higher rates of central assistance for particular schemes. There was also no concerted effort in the formulation of an integrated economic development programme for agriculture and allied fields. Thus the development efforts of the first three plan periods did not produce any perceptible impact on the economic life of the people in such backward and inaccessible regions.

During the Fourth Plan, the economic development of the backward areas were looked upon as essentially the responsibility of the State Governments. The Central Government only took some limited selective measures to help solve particular problems in some selected backward areas. Some weightage was also given to the less developed states in the allocation of central assistance to meet the special needs and problems of the weaker sections. The basic objective of the Fifth Plan has been the removal of poverty and attainment of economic self-reliance. Accelerated development of the backward areas is necessary to reduce regional imbalances.

Most of the hill areas in the country have remained comparatively neglected due to the difficult terrain and absence of communications. This backwardness is not always due to lack of natural resources, but largely due to neglect and lack of concerted attention. The economy of a backward region like Kumaun Division, which is comprised of the typical backward hill districts of U.P. can be transformed into a prosperous and flourishing one with proper attention, adequate investment and adoption of the right strategy of development.

Scope of Integrated Rural Development

"Until not long ago - and this view tends to persist-the term development was used to refer to economic growth. But the importance of non-economic dimensions

11. Ibid, para IV. 16.

of development, political, social, cultural and human, is being increasingly realised now."[12] Another view is that "development is the process whereby human beings try to shape and reshape the natural environment."[13] In fact, the term development implies a process of change and improvement. The change is for better results from a co-ordinated, continuing and purposive activity of: (1) the people; (2) their government; and (3) the appropriate technical and professional services.[14] It is not necessary for these forces to be simultaneously present from the start in order that development may take place. Each has in itself the capacity to produce some change. But when all the three work in combination, the results are more lasting and have a different stamp. Awareness of this by workers at all levels helps to make for better team work.

Rural development is generally conceived as a multi-sectoral activity which includes besides agricultural development, rural industries, the establishment or improvement of social overhead facilities or infra-structure, such as schools, clinics, roads, communication, water supply, markets, welfare sources, improved nutrition, literacy, adult education, etc. The primary object of rural development is the enrichment of the quality of life of the rural masses, particularly the poorer and the weaker sections of the rural society.

The term 'Integrated Rural Development' in recent years has received general acceptance by politicians, administrators, social workers, economists and scientists. This term is taken to mean a 'package programme'. "It must take account of the inter-relationship of socio-political, economic and technical factors in a system's approach."[15] I.R.D. is, and will continue to be, the central theme in our programmes of rural uplift. It necessarily involves the use of science and technology by the masses for the betterment of their socio-economic conditions or their development, and the improvement in the quality of life. The village offers the best location and the focus of all programmes of I.R.D.

I.R.D. is the accepted strategy for the development of rural areas in the nation's Sixth Five-Year-Plan. The dual objective of rural development which has been undivided by the Planning Commission is : (1) increase of production in agriculture and allied sectors, and (2) generation of employment. Special emphasis has also been laid in the current plan on the development of target groups comprising small and marginal farmers, agricultural labourers and rural artisans

---

12. Sharma, S.L.: Criteria of Social Development, Social Action,, IN ISBN 0037-7627, Jan-March 1980, Vol. 30, No. 1, p. 62
13. Sharma, Sudesh Kumar.: Dynamics of Development, Delhi, Concept Publishing Company, 1977, p. 3.
14. Action for Rural Change, Readings in Indian Community Development, New Delhi, Munshiram Manoharlal Publishers, 1970, p. 271.
15. Kotter, H.R.: "Some Observation on Basic Principles and General Strategy Under Statics" Vol. 13, No. 4, 1974.

who either do not own land or have quite inadequate land holdings in their possession. In order to achieve the above objectives, optimum utilization of land, water and human resources have been emphasized.

According to S.K. Rau "the concept of integrated rural development is being variously interpreted in different quarters. Some consider it as one of the many programmes of rural development, thus equating it with programmes of SFDA/ MFAL. Others think that is the refurnished version of old community development programme. In either case, the objectives of the I.R.D. and the new approach it advocates are getting diluted. There is, therefore, a need to emphasize the totality of approach under I.R.D. comprehending the entire gamut of rural development programmes currently under implementation. It has to be appreciated that this programme envisages a comprehensive approach to rural development focussed on channelling benefits to the rural poor."[16] The concept of I.R.D. also encompasses rural industrialization and formation of new skills activating and modernizing the traditional ones so that rural artisans would benefit under this programme. Further, I.R.D. should be people's programme with enough built-in mechanism to produce more wealth and distribute it among the selected beneficiaries and effectively associate the beneficiaries with the process of production and distribution.

I.R.D. also aims at development which can help to increase the purchasing power of the rural poor through generation of greater opportunities for gainful employment. The rural poor include small and marginal farmers, landless labourers, working women and rural artisans whose level of living is below the subsistence level.

"Conceptually, I.R.D. should mean multi-faced development of rural economy by exploiting to the optimum the local resources in men, material, land and water. It has to be mainly on the basis of local initiative and drive. The Government should act as a catalyst to bring about this change but it is the intrinsic strength of the economy itself which should support the services, the rising standards and sectoral economic activities. This concept brings out the importance of integrating all economic activities in consonance with the local resources. The vast untapped rural labour force is a liability which has to be turned into assets by harnessing them in fruitful and gainful employment. Full rural employment is the goal of I.R.D."[17]

Thus I.R.D. envisages an all round development of the rural areas with the objective of banishing poverty and unemployment. The ultimate objective is to improve the quality of life in rural areas. It is a strategy to improve the economic and social life of the rural masses in the overall spectrum of development and

16. Rau, S.K.: Integrated Rural Development, Rural Development Digest, Vol. 3, Jan. 1980, No. 1, p. 31.
17. Arora, R.C.: Integrated Rural Development, New Delhi, S. Chand and Company Ltd., 1977, pp. 3-4.

growth. The keynote is that it is not only improvement to raise the agricultural productivity and the rate of overall economic growth in rural areas, but also that it has to be ensured that the poorer and the weaker sections in rural localities share its benefits. In short, "the overall concern is on community orientation, minimum state intervention, mass participation, self-reliance, non-specialization, pooling of local resources and service to the people." Thus, "I.R.D. has been defined as development and utilization of local resources—physical, biological and human—by bringing out necessary institutional, structural and attitudinal changes with the ultimate objective of improving the quality of life of the poor. The agency to implement such programmes must cover agriculture and allied sectors, small and cottage industries, health and educational programmes, environmental improvements, community welfare, etc. The agency should have the over-view of all the elements involved in rural development. It should be able to formulate its programmes, draw out the priorities and should have the operational freedom to execute them."[18] Therefore, I.R.D. aims at total development of the area and the people by bringing about the necessary institutional and attitudinal changes and by delivering a package of services through extensive methods to encompass not only the economic field, e.g. development of agriculture and rural industries, etc. but also the establishment of the required special infra-structure and services in the area of health and nutrition, education and literacy, basic civic amenities, family welfare, etc. with the ultimate objective of improving the quality of life in rural areas.

"I.R.D. envisages a multi-disciplinary approach in which all disciplines and organisations work in a coordinated way at all levels from the top floor to the ground level, to develop better insights in the appraisal and use of human, animal, plant, soil, water and mineral resources, to understand the constraints in their full use and to suggest appropriate action plan for their optimum use for increasing income, production and employment with social justice in rural areas."[19] The I.R.D. plan, therefore, necessitates flexibility. No uniformity should be imposed on a situation which is essentially diverse, heterogeneous and does not lead to uniform method and paths of development. Another important requirement of I.R.D. plan is that the programmes and schemes be located and identified by the villagers themselves. These should be thoroughly discussed, modified, doubted and dissented by the villagers themselves. The single sure test of success of I.R.D. plan should be the extent to which it realizes the creative potentialities of rural masses.

---

18. Arora, R.C.: Integrated Rural Development, New Delhi, S. Chand and Company Ltd., 1977, p. 340.
19. Resource Inventory and I.R.D. Plan for Tehri Garhwal District (Project Report), G.P. Pant University, Pantnagar, 1976.

In short, the objectives of I.R.D. may be summarized as follows:

1. Maximization of production in agriculture and allied sectors as well as in rural industries.
2. Generation of employment in rural areas with particular emphasis on increasing the income and employment opportunities for those living below the poverty line.
3. To integrate the agricultural and non-agricultural plans in such a way that the surplus manpower from the agricultural sector is absorbed in the non-agricultural sector.
4. To develop better insights in the appraisal and use of human, animal, plant, soil, water, mineral and other resources of the area concerned.
5. To improve the living condition, nutrition and health of the rural poor.

"In order to achieve the objectives of I.R.D., it is essential to revamp the implementation machinery which should not only break the inertia of the people and the democratic institutions but should also have the necessary authority, flexibility and wherewithal to execute the programmes. Care has also to be taken to ensure that there is no further proliferation of bureaucracy and that the existing institutions, agencies, staff are fully utilised with such modifications that might be compelling and are considered inevitable to meet the complexities of the situations."[20] The strength and weakness of the present structure must be objectively assessed before suggesting the changes to achieve the objective of I.R.D. Whilst there must be great and, in fact, predominant emphasis upon the poorer sections in planning and implementation, integration can only mean a process of planning and management which embraces all the governmental activities related to the economic and social well-being of the rural areas. Thus, I.R.D. recognizes that the problem of poverty, unemployment and underemployment in rural areas are not likely to be solved through ad hoc and isolated sectoral programmes. It also lays emphasis on optimum utilization of local resources—human, biological and natural—through the inputs of science and technology for the benefit of the rural poor and the disadvantaged groups.

I.R.D. is not merely a programme of rural development, but an umbrella under which all rural development programmes are integrated. Essentially, the programme embodies an approach of achieving rural development. All the programmes currently under implementation need to be brought together under one programme and attempts need to be made to identify and fill the gaps in them providing personnel and improving the organizational structure and other arrangements considered necessary and suitable.

---

20. Arora, R.C.: op. cit. p. 339.

Its Significance in India

'India lives in villages' is an established fact. But during a long long period of its political foreign domination the village communities remained neglected in all walks of life. During the freedom movement of the present era, it was in the writings and deeds of Gandhiji, Father of the Nation, that greatest emphasis was laid upon their uplift. Hence, as soon as India became Independent, the problem of rural development as the first priority drew the attention of our policy makers, planners and administrators. But, even after about three decades of planned development the results achieved have not been upto the desired expectations. Various reasons may be cited for such situation. One important reason is that most of our developmental programmes were often planned and implemented in a fragmented and compartmented approach and the importance of understanding the totality of the situation was not considered as a prerequisite. Even in the agricultural field which is the core of rural development, the integrated approach remained lacking. The recent emphasis on integrated area development is the result of increasing concern over the unsatisfactory state of affairs with regard to the spatial distribution and levels of socio-economic facilities in the rural areas. The urgent need to correct this situation is self-evident.

Three special programmes, namely S.F.D.A., D.P.A.P. and C.A.D. are being implemented in a number of blocks in the country. "In the Fourth Plan, two schemes of S.F.D.A. and M.F.A.L. were introduced for making the small and marginal farmers economically viable and for improving the lot of landless agricultural labourers by raising the output of small holdings and generating employment through subsidiary occupations."[21] The main objective was to reach the benefits of agricultural development to the numerically large but economically weaker sections of the rural community.

"In the Fifth Plan, the two schemes of S.F.D.A. and M.F.A.L. were merged and the number of projects increased to 960."[22] The programmes undertaken in the SFDA—MFAL projects include both land-based and animal husbandry programmes. With the object of providing development investments in areas where drought has been a recurring feature, a Rural Works Programme was initiated in 1970-71 in an attempt to mitigate the scarcity conditions of those areas. In the Fifth Plan, the scheme was reoriented as an area development programme under the name 'Drought Prone Area Programme'. "The strategy is to improve the economy of the drought prone areas through a package of infra-structural and on-farm development

21. Guidelines for Intensive Development of Blocks under the Programme for I.R.D., Vol. II. (Annexes), New Delhi, Ministry of Agriculture and Irrigation, Govt. of India, 1978, p. 1.
22. Ibid, p. 1.

activities with the objective of optimum utilization of land, water, human and livestock resources of the area."[23]

With the spurt in the construction of major and medium irrigation works after Independence and consequent increase in the commands of the irrigation works, the need for realizing faster and optimum utilization of the irrigation potential created was keenly felt. With this objective in view, the Command Area Development Scheme was introduced in December, 1974. The programme also lays emphasis on various on-farm development activities with special emphasis on the weaker sections being unable to take full part therein.

Out of about, 5,000 Blocks in the country, approximately 3,000 blocks are covered by one or more of the Special Programmes mentioned above. The blocks were selected on certain considerations relevant to the states and the area concerned. The Government of India had undertaken a review of the working of these programmes all over the country and come to the conclusion that a programme of intensive and I.R.D. should be undertaken in 2,000 out of the 3,000 blocks covered by any one or more of these programmes.

The fact has now come to be realized that isolated attempts and ad hoc projects or schemes cannot ultimately solve the problem of the rural weak. This is why a new emphasis is being laid on I.R.D. in favour of rural poverty and backwardness. At present, almost the whole of rural India has been covered by Village Panchayats. The cooperative movement and I.R.D. plans have also been forging ahead. If democratic socialism is to be realized, its base will have to be the rural sector. We are progressing towards a society which is predominantly agricultural. Panchayats and cooperatives are the instruments for realizing democratic socialism. The purpose is to provide every village with an opportunity to produce more, to learn more, to earn more, to consume more and, as a result, to enjoy better living

Gandhiji emphatically taught his countrymen the philosophy of ruralism. He was deadly opposed to heavy industrialization which meant the extensive use of machinery resulting, according to him, in the problem of mass unemployment. The rural areas are the main sources of essential supplies - food for people, raw material for industries, construction material for houses, and so on. In villages beats the pulse of India. The neglect of villages will result in extreme poverty in rural areas and a very wide gap between the income of a villager and that of a city dweller. Therefore, it is but natural that highest priority should be given to rural development.

Gandhiji has a semi-mystical vision of the village and ascribed to his idealized community the qualities he sought to inspire in the India of his dreams. His

23. Ibid, p. 2.

philosophy drawn from Tolstoy and Kropotkin, rejected the modern state as a foreign accretion upon the true India which he regarded as a federation of village republics or Panchayati Raj. "That state will be best which is governed the least"[24] declared Gandhiji, and "society based on non-violence can only consist of groups settled in villages in which voluntary cooperation is the pre-condition of dignified and peaceful existence...The nearest approach to civilisation based on non-violence is the erstwhile village republic in India."[25]

The teachings of Gandhiji who pleaded for decentralization and a "return to the villages", had prepared for decades the minds of people to the belief that 'Swaraj' would have no meaning or content, unless and until it reached the far-flung villages. Independence will have to begin at the bottom, so that every village would have a republic or panchayat having full powers. It is agreed that the Indian village throughout ages has been a corporate body, guided and guarded by a council, the panchayat. There is tacit agreement that the functioning of the panchayat provided a kind of prelude to democracy.

The conclusion which generally follows is that the village republic must be revived as the foundation of the new India. It is a living tradition from which grows grassroots of democracy that is native to Indian soil. In the present days India believes in the village as the political bedrock stems. Some forty years ago, Indian political theorists, looking back to their past, considered the village only as the base of royal authority. But today, they view the ancient village as a self-governing community.

Village Panchayats and Community Development Programmes

With the implementation of the recommendations of the C.O.P.P., Panchayati Raj institutions have become the institutions of democratic-decentralization at the grassroot levels and the vehicles of the Community Development movement. Our late Prime Minister, Pandit Jawaharlal Nehru made this very clear when he said, "The Community Projects appear to me something of vital importance not only for the material achievement that they would bring about, but much more so, because they seem to build up the community and the individual and to make the latter the builder of his own village, centres and of India in the larger sense." Quite appropriately, therefore, extension has been chosen to be the method and community development, the aim of India's Community Development Programme. S.K. Dey rightly observes "Community Development is the end. Panchayati Raj is the means."

24. Agarwal, S.N. : Gandhian Constitution for Free India, Allahabad, Kitabistan, 1946, p. 39..
25. Ibid, p. 58.

Since the launching of the Community Development Programme in 1952 and the introduction of Panchayati Raj— "there are 5026 Community Development Blocks and 2, 22, 055 village Panchayats in India"[26] - of these in Kumaun Division there are 39 Community Development Blocks and 2700 Village Panchayats, the endeavour has been to create a suitable climate and provide a viable infrastructure for all round development in the rural areas.

Community Development in a sense aims at achieving the aims of *Sarvodaya*. It is the common goal of all who believe in the doctrine of a socialist society. "Community development implies the emergence of individuals out of a given mass, enjoying peace and prosperity. It is such individuals who will constitute a community, that will throw up not merely political leaders but perfect leaders; and a state led by such leaders will have no occasion, perhaps, to whither itself away."[27] Another important aspect of C.D. is its tenet that the community is the basic unit of development.[28] This means an integrated development of the total community life. Otherwise, the programme would be compartmentalized. Thus, C.D. has been described as "a movement designed to promote better living for the whole community with the active participation and initiative of the community."

In our country, during the independence movement, organized efforts for rural development were initiated by voluntary organizations and individuals. After Independence, the government launched a massive programme of Community Development by associating it with Panchayati Raj institutions and various other popular agencies for its effective implementation. In spite of the gigantic efforts made under the Community Development Programme and under various plan projects, the villages, by and large, have remained backward and the rural people still suffer from serious deprivation—social, economic and political. Illiteracy, lack of sanitation, inadequate supply of potable water, lack of medical and educational facilities, poor housing, underemployment and above all, the tradition bound attitudes continue to keep the rural masses in a state of lethargy. "While Community Development must contribute to strengthening the economic base, its more significant contribution is in providing the conditions for improving the quality of human life. The objective of Community Development and, therefore, the basis on which it should be judged must be the contribution it makes in developing the competence of village people to function effectively as individuals and in democratic institutions fostering and giving leadership to integrated rural development."[29]

---

26. Rural Development Programme in India, New Delhi, Ministry of Agriculture and Irrigation, Government of India, 1978, p. 1.
27. Haq, M.S.: Community Development through Extension, Allahabad, Chugh Publication, 1979, p. 138.
28. Bhattacharyya, S.N.: Community Development, Calcutta, Academic Publishers, 1970.
29. Ensminger Douglas: Rural India in Transition, New Delhi, Thomson Press (India) Limited, 1972, p. 84.

The problem of community development in these backward and under-developed hill districts needs immediate attention. The amount of money to be spent by a block on developmental schemes, in case of these hill districts should be comparatively larger in view of the fact that the cost of executing work projects in the hills is higher than that in the plains, and that these underdeveloped areas need more schemes of village improvement. The territorial jurisdiction of a block in these hills has been quite big and the development officers posted in these blocks do not find adequate opportunities to supervise the work of different panchayats. Greater emphasis has to be laid upon the desirability of curtailing frequent meetings of block officials at the block and district headquarters, as it is an unnecessary wastage of time and money, and results in the absence of these officials from the field stations where they are greatly needed.

The villagers and the peasants, in the present conditions, can make the best use of their available resources through cooperation. "In the Community Development approach, the objective is to work for and with the village people and in the technical ministries, single purpose approach, the village people would be expected to work for objectives set by the outside technical ministries and agencies. One is a response to the people's interest and needs; the other is to get the people to respond to what the outside agencies determine to be the village priorities and with what money they have to spend in the village."[30] In fact, cooperation is the basis of the entire Community Development Programme. Its aim of socio-economic uplift can be achieved only through cooperative effort. Community Development can be put on a sound foundation only when there is a network of cooperative farms, service cooperative societies and other cooperatives.

The general purpose of such programmes is to bring about social and economic improvements and to integrate the communities into the national life. More specific objectives of specific programmes include improving health, nutrition, agricultural production, establishing and/or improving handicrafts industries, marketing arrangements, means of communication and public utilities, raising the level of literacy, and so on. These objectives involve changes in the behaviour, beliefs and attitudes of the members of the community and may involve changes in their established network of relations. Community development may be seen as goal oriented change.

According to the principle of community development, such change should not be imposed from above, but should be effected through the active involvement and participation of the panchayats and community members. "No high-pressure methods should be used. Discovery and development of local leadership as well

30. Ensminger Dougals: Rural India in Transition, New Delhi, Thomson Press (India) Limited, 1972, p. 29.

as voluntary participation and decision making by the local people in the choice of the programmes, planning and execution should be the keynotes, persuasion and motivation being the only tools in the hands of the project workers, who should work, not for or on the people, but with and through them. In the long run, Community Development should become a people's programme with Government participation and not vice versa."[31] This demands their recognition that the projected change will indeed improve their lives and add to their material and spiritual well-being. Such recognition may not be easily forthcoming, for many deeply embedded traditions and social arrangements may be challenged by the new ideas and projected activities.

The involvement of the rural people in schemes for the development of their resources and the general improvement of their living conditions was, and remains, the essential purpose of the C.D. and N.E. movement, inaugurated on Gandhiji's birthday in October 1952. "Community development is both paternal and democratic - paternal in the sense that the initiative in breaking the 'cake of custom' comes from above and that most of the 'know-how' and many of the resources are supplied from outside; democratic in the sense that progress is achieved through the enlistment of the willing consent and active participation of the people themselves. Its ultimate objective is a self-liquidating one, to be achieved when the process of development becomes self-generating and self-sustaining."[32]

Unless the Panchayat office-bearers and the village people come in frequent and direct contact with the Development staff, the emergence of village leadership, which is very essential for initiating and completing the plans of village development by the people themselves, is not possible. The officials of the blocks must not adopt a bossing attitude but should be imbued with the weal of service to the people.

"The principal objective of C.D. is to bring about social and economic advancement through the creation of new psychological attitudes. In essence it is a psychological process intended to wean the village people from their reliance on the traditions of the past and to create in them a full acceptance of science and technology in their ways both of living and making a living."[33]

If the philosophy of village level democracy is to succeed, then it is surely important that Community Development movement itself should faithfully reflect the levelling down of the locus of power to the village level. Even today the first necessity is to make the development programme a people's programme. It is still

31. Singh, D.P.: 'The Pilot Development Project, Etawa', in Evolution of C.D. Programme, pp. 55, 56.
32. Hanson, A.H.: The Process of Planning: A Study of India's Five-Year Plans 1950-64, London, Oxford University Press, 1966, p. 420.
33. Ensminger Douglas: Democratic Decentralisation: A New Administrative Challenge, The Indian Journal of Public Administration, July-September, 1961, Vol. VII, No. 3.

very much a Government programme. This is the chief reason for the comparatively poor results achieved from the Community Development in spite of huge expenditures incurred on it. Since all the people do not extend whole-hearted cooperation in devising and executing the Community Development plans, the integrated rural development cannot progress. Community development can be real only when the community understands its own problems and realizes its responsibilities in solving these problems. The village panchayats as the representatives of community would be the only agency that can shoulder this responsibility effectively.

Importance of Village Panchayats in I.R.D.

The most pressing problem in India today is that of improving the economic and social condition of the vast number of people in rural areas who live below the poverty line. Socio-economic development of rural area is of crucial significance in the framework of integrated growth and social justice. "of the three major elements, the social structure of Indian society, the village is most important in the programme of rural development. The village, however, is the grassroots organization through which the Community Development Extension Programme is expected to operate. This is because India is a society of villages and will be for decades to come."[34] Sir Charles, writing in 1832, said, "The village communities are little republics, having nearly everything they want within themselves, and almost independent of any foreign relations. They seem to last where nothing else lasts."[35]

In the post-Independence period, a great deal of attention is being paid to the reorganization of village panchayats and to facilitate decentralization of power and responsibility. In the Constituent Assembly, some members emphatically observed that the Constitution should have been drafted entirely on ancient Hindu model of a State and should have given Village Panchayats the status of the foundations of the State structure.[36]

Without giving the village panchayats their due importance it is very difficult to solve the problems of I.R.D. In the true democracy of India, the unit was the village. Even if one village wanted Panchayati Raj, which was called republic in English, no one could stop it. "True democracy could not be worked by twenty

34. Taylor, Carl C., Ensminger, D., Johnson, Helen W., Jean Joyce; India's Roots of Democracy, Calcutta, Orient Longmans, 1965, p. 29.
35. Metcalfe, Sir Charles, Report of the Select Committee of the House of Commons, 1832, Vol. III, Appendix 84, p. 331. Cited in Srinivas, M.N. (Ed.), India's Villages.
36. Venktarangia, M. Pattabhiram; Local Government in India (Edited) Bombay-1, Allied Publishers, p. 248, 1969.

men sitting at the Centre. It had to be worked from below by the people of every village."[37] Democracy does not merely mean Parliament at the top or in the States, but something which means a representative that excites every person and something that trains every one to take his proper place and indeed any place in the country if need arise. Village panchayats should not be mere formal statutory bodies but should be real and effective representative bodies invested with sufficient powers of planning and execution of the schemes of rural development. Side by side, adequate financial powers should also be devolved upon them. Rural development and rural welfare are possible only through local initiative and discretion. The First Five Year Plan rightly observed: "We believe that the Panchayats will be able to perform their civic functions satisfactorily only if these are associated with an active process of development in which the village panchayat itself gives an effective part. Unless a village agency assumes responsibility and initiative for developing the resources of the village, it will be difficult to make impression on rural life, for only a village organization representing the community as a whole can provide the necessary leadership. As the agencies of State Government cannot easily approach each individual villager separately progress depends largely on the existence of an active organization in the village which can bring the people into common programmes to be carried out with the assistance of the administration."[38] With the inauguration of the three tier structure of rural local self-government and community development in the countryside, the panchayat institutions are expected to serve as the most vital instruments of I.R.D.

"I.R.D. is, and will continue to be, the central theme in the nation's programmes of rural uplift. The conventional exponential growth model which has been adopted by some countries has dangerous limitations and, as is well realized, it cannot apply to the developing countries like India, which have to evolve their own models where the central thrust is to reduce poverty and misery that abounds in the rural areas. The purpose is also to lay the foundation of the new society with due emphasis on balanced equilibrium of human and ecological resources. It necessarily involves the use of science and technology by the masses in the betterment of their socio-economic conditions or their development and the improvement in the quality of life."[39] The village panchayats offer the best location and the focus of all programmes of I.R.D.

In order to provide each individual citizen of the Indian countryside with

---

37. Gandhi, M.K.: *Harijan*, 18 January, 1948, quoted in, Report of the Fourth National Conference, AIPP.
38. Op. cit, p. 333
39. Quoted from the Speech of Sri S.P. Pande, (V.C.): Regional-Seminar on Planning for Integrated Rural Development, March 30 and 31, 1977, G.B. Pant University of Agriculture and Technology, Pantnagar.

opportunities to evolve himself through his own selected medium in social, economic cultural and political spheres of life, the system of rural local self-government would be of prime importance, so that an average citizen may not remain merely a passive participant, casting his vote indifferently and unintelligently. The village panchayats would serve as the basic units of that system. For the achievement of the objectives laid down in the Constitution,[40] the village panchayats will have to serve not only as units of local self-government, but also as natural institutions for securing social justice and fostering corporate life resulting in full employment.[41]

Most Indians are subject to a whole series of interlocking communities, but the only territorial tie that is really compulsive is the village. It is true that the district and the state are both important, but the village is the sheet-anchor of a man's sense of place and of home. Of the three tiers of the new structure, the Gaon Panchayat must be the solid foundation and the village community must be the source of the authority of Gaon panchayats. If the village panchayats are to be the base of I.R.D., the members of the village panchayat need to be very alert and conscious about their rights and obligations. Youth, both men and women, will have to play the most dynamic role in the new dispensation.

The transformation of Indian rural masses into a 'Socialistic Pattern of Society' for the solution of their socio-economic problems, is possible only through a non-violent process by a progressive creation of a network of village panchayats, enabling them to participate in the administration and community development programmes of rural reconstruction. These systems would help to evolve local leadership and corporate life, and mobilize local resources and potentialities in rural life which are so very essential for carrying out the programmes of I.R.D.

Importance of I.R.D. in Kumaun Hills

The importance of launching the programme of I.R.D. in areas having peculiar geographical and socio-economic conditions deserves special consideration. Kumaun Division comprising the hill district of Almora, Nainital and Pithoragarh in Uttar Pradesh has such peculiar geographical and socio-economic features. The vast population of this area resides in small habitations known as villages. They are economically very backward and the topographical conditions prevailing in these hill districts need special attention for rural development. The population of these three districts, blockwise has been shown in the tables below:

40. Article 39.
41. Cf.: Report of Congress Village Panchayat Committee, 1954, All India Congress Committee Office, New Delhi, p. 16.

TABLE - 1

STATISTICAL DATA OF POPULATION - DISTRICT ALMORA[42]

Sl. No.	Name of the Block	Total No. of Villages	Uninhabited Villages	Villages with population of Less than 200 (Nos)	200-499 (Nos)	500-999 (Nos)	1000-1999 (Nos)
1.	Bhainsiachhna	131	4	80	39	7	1
2.	Dhauladevi	242	9	154	65	13	1
3.	Hawalbagh	229	23	116	73	16	1
4.	Lamgarha	207	19	181	47	10	-
5.	Bageshwar	384	30	269	76	9	-
6.	Garur	189	3	166	62	16	2
7.	Kapkote	214	13	107	70	18	6
8.	Takula	231	20	129	63	17	2
9.	Bhikiasen	202	14	112	67	9	-
10.	Chaukhutia	171	7	83	61	20	-
11.	Dwarahat	216	10	105	76	19	6
12.	Salt	253	14	161	79	9	-
13.	Syalde	193	6	108	60	19	-
14.	Tarikhet	267	10	155	90	11	1
15.	Forest Charge	5	-	5	-	-	-
District Total		3134	172	1321	928	193	20

Total Population = 6,48,729

Urban Population = 39,252
Rural Population = 6,09,477

42. Statistical Booklet, Office of the Statistics Officer, Almora, State Planning Department, Finance and Statistics Division, 1978, U.P.

TABLE - 2

STATISTICAL DATA OF POPULATION - DISTRICT PITHORAGARH[43]

Sl. No.	Name of the Block	Total No. of Villages	Uninhabited Villages (Nos)	Villages with population of Less than 200 (Nos)	200-499 (Nos)	500-999 (Nos)	1000-1499 (Nos)	1500-1999 (Nos)
1.	Kanalichanna	207	5	134	61	6	1	-
2.	Digttar	168	4	110	46	6	2	-
3.	Berinag	282	15	209	52	60	-	-
4.	Dharchula	658	24	19	31	10	5	5
5.	Pithoragarh	164	6	86	55	16	1	-
6.	Gangolihat	325	28	208	70	19	-	-
7.	Munakot	173	8	102	47	10	-	-
8.	Munchari	223	5	158	50	4	1	-
9.	Champawat	259	23	177	54	4	1	-
10.	Barakot	192	9	120	53	10	-	-
11.	Lohaghat	205	15	135	46	7	1	1
	District Total	2857	142	1458	565	152	12	6

Total Population = 4,15,163

43. Statistical Booklet, Office of the Statistics Officer, Pithoragarh, State Planning Department, Finance and Statistics Division, 1979, U.P.

TABLE - 3

STATISTICAL DATA OF POPULATION - DISTRICT NAINITAL[44]

Sl. No.	Name of the Block	Total No. of Villages	Uninhabited Villages (Nos)	Villages with population of Less than 200 (Nos)	200-499 (Nos)	500-999 (Nos)	1000-1499 (Nos)	1500-1999 (Nos)
1.	Okhalkanda	120	1	68	44	7	-	-
2.	Betalghat	168	10	107	43	8	-	-
3.	Ramgarh	159	6	103	36	10	4	-
4.	Bhimtal	131	4	78	31	14	3	1
	Total = (Hill Blocks)	578	21	356	154	39	7	1
5.	Haldwani	289	5	202	68	8	5	1
6.	Ramnagar	212	3	152	39	15	2	1
7.	Kashipur	177	10	52	66	31	11	6
8.	Bajpur/ Gadarpur	195	3	59	61	49	9	14
9.	Rudrapur	92	4	23	24	25	10	18
10.	Khatima	245	10	48	94	73	11	13
	District Total	1788	56	688	506	240	55	54

Total Population = 7,90,080

Urban Population = 17,4,879
Rural Population = 6,15,201

N.B: Figures in respect of Blocks at Nos. 5 to 10 relate to the area covering Bhabar, Tarai and plains portions of the District.

The geographical conditions have largely determined the composition of population in these hill districts. According to the census of 1971, the percentage of rural and urban population in Kumaun was 87.81 and 12.79 respectively as shown below :

44. Statistical Booklet, Office of the Statistics Officer, Nainital, State Planning Department, Finance and Statistics Division, 1979, U.P.

TABLE - 4

PERCENTAGE DISTRIBUTION OF THE POPULATION OF KUMAUN CLASSIFIED INTO RURAL-URBAN CATEGORIES IN LAST THREE CENSUSES[45]

Figure in percent

	1951		1961		1971	
District	Rural	Urban	Rural	Urban	Rural	Urban
Almora	95.46	4.54	95.50	4.50	94.79	5.21
Pithoragarh	-	-	100.00	0.00	96.19	3.81
Nainital	77.44	22.06	180.47	19.53	77.87	22.13
Total Kumaun	89.11	10.79	89.54	10.46	87.81	12.19

Total table shows that there has been a gradual increase in the urban population of Kumaun since 1951. However, it showed a decrease in 1961. This is due to the fact, that a large number of immigrants settled in the bhabar and tarai rural areas of Nainital district and reduced the ratio of urban population to the total population. The highest growth rate in urban population over the last three decades was recorded in district Pithoragarh, particularly after 1961. This was due to the growth of townships in the district, in view of the newly created headquarters for the border district and considerable attention being paid by the Government in this district regarding opening hospitals, educational institutions, markets and other administrative services. Urban-rural categories are a matter of definitions and the urban features are generated by emergence of civic services by the State. Military headquarters in Pithoragarh has also helped the process of urbanization considerably.

Taking into consideration the existing low-level of development of the natural and human resources and their potential for further development for the betterment of rural folk of this typically backward area, a vigorous and well-devised plan for I.R.D. needs to be launched. It is only through an integrated approach to the problems of the village communities that a perceptible improvement can be brought about in the living conditions of these hill districts.

Although vast sums of money are spent through the development blocks on various schemes, yet the results are far from satisfactory. Kumaun Division has a secluded type of economy with the background of uneven topography. The means of communication and transport are very insufficient. Although, the quantum of total per capita land available in the hill area is higher than in the plains yet here, a major part of the total area is either covered by forests or is rocky. The

45. District Census Handbooks of the respective districts for 1951, 1961 and 1971.

geographical area and land utilization of these three districts is represented by the table below.

TABLE - 5

AREA AND LAND UTILIZATION[46]

Districts	Geographical Area in sq.km	Agricultural area sown In Hectares	Culturable Waste Hectares	Forest Hectares	Area not available for agricultural in Hectares: Pastures Pastures or grazing grounds	Orchard
Almora	546097	123765	12937	288953	41800	9368
Nainital	6792	200995	30963	398449	1037	19750
Pithoragarh	8885	71552	51807	330569	7710	-

Thus in the whole Kumaun Division only 23 per cent of the total area is available for cultivation. The rest is either covered with dense forests or is otherwise not available for cultivation. Then, there is the problem of soil conservation. All this results in very low productivity from agricultural land. The perfunctory existence and functional short-coming of canals and lack of regular and assured water supply constitute a bottle-neck in the growth of intensive crop production. Thus, the scope of agriculture is very meagre. But on the other hand, horticulture can play an important role in the economy of this hill area. The agro-climatic conditions in areas at higher altitude are more favourable for growing temperate fruits and raising the off-season vegetables too.

Kumaun hills with its forests, flora and fauna, its geology, mineral resources, climate and overall scenic beauty, offer potentialities of development of forest based industries like soap making, copper and iron vessels, woollen goods like carpet, sweaters and other clothes, tourism, cement, herbs, etc.

In Kumaun hills, the community life is also of secluded type, because the village sites are scattered. Since the villages in these hills are situated either in the valleys, on the banks of the hilly rivers, or on the slopes of small hills, the problems of the village communities residing in these hills are quite different from their prototypes in the plains. In the northern parts of these hills, the scattered villages are like oases in these mountain deserts which are too rugged and too cold for profitable cultivation.[47] Hence, the plans of rural development in these hill districts

46. Statistical Booklets, Office of the Statistics Officer, Almora, Nainital, Pithoragarh; State Planning Department, Finance and Statistics Division, 1979, U.P.
47. Cf. Pant S.D.: Social Economy of the Himalayas, London, George Allen and Unwin Ltd., 1935, p. 42.

need some special orientation taking all these factors into consideration. They cannot be followed in these hill districts exactly as in plains. Therefore, an identical policy in planning for I.R.D. in respect of the plains and the hills would not be desirable in view of the special geographical conditions and requirements obtaining in the hill countryside. The policy of creating of Special Planning body for hill districts and training the personnel of development blocks of these areas on the lines specially suited for hills will have to be adopted. Developmental schemes of agriculture, cooperative industries, and even the construction works in these hills need differential treatment as regards their planning and execution. The developmental schemes for the hill areas would be different in many respects from those outlined for U.P. as a whole. They need special emphasis on the improvement of communication, development of horticulture, rural industries, community forests, village cooperative societies, etc.

The development of the rural communities in these hill villages, from the angle of science and technology, is also very necessary to improve the rural community life. Therefore, I.R.D. programmes need some different orientation for the uplift of socio-economic conditions of these people. The Kumaun hills are lagging far behind in the scientific knowledge, proper planning, management and development of their natural resources. Science and modern technology have yet to make their impact in natural resource utilization for increasing income and quality of life. The theme 'Science and Integrated Rural Development' aims at making optimum use of available local resources through purposive inputs of science and technology for rural development. It is now felt that planning needs to be resource-oriented and science and technology should be brought to bear their impact in the appraisal and development of natural resources.

2

ORGANIZATION OF PANCHAYATI RAJ BODIES IN KUMAUN

Implementation of U.P. Panchayati Raj Act in Kumaun

The U.P. Panchayati Raj Act, 1947 was enacted with the object of "establishing and development Local Self-Government in the rural areas of U.P., and to make better provision for village administration and development."[1] It provides for the establishment of a net work of village panchayats in the whole countryside of the State and makes provision for the organization, powers, finances, direction, supervision and control of these bodies.

The U.P. Panchayati Raj Amendment Act Committee, 1953 was appointed to suggest ways and means for further amendment of the Act with a view to establish democratic institutions in an efficient and systematic way through which people could be entrusted with the responsibility of Local Self-Government and administration of justice.[2]

The Committee submitted its report in 1954, and upon its recommendation, the U.P. Panchayati Raj Amendment Bill, 1952 was introduced in the Legislature and enacted in following year.[3] The existing Panchayat system is based upon the provisions of this amended Act which came in force on 1.4.1956. Since then several minor amendments have also been enacted from time to time to suit the exigencies necessitated for its enforcement.[4]

Organization of Panchayats in Kumaun

Under the U.P. Panchayati Raj Act as amended from time to time there is a three-fold organization of panchayat bodies: the Gaon Sabha constitute the primary village assembly, the Gaon Panchayat acts as the executive committee of the Gaon Sabha and the Nyaya Panchayat is the village tribunal entrusted with administration of justice in petty disputes of villagers.

1. Cf. Preamble to the Act.
2. Cf. *Report of the U.P. Panchayat Raj Amendment Act Committee*, 1954, Lucknow, Supdt. Ptg. and Sty., U.P., 1954, pp. 2-3.
3. U.P. Act II of 1955.
4. U.P. Act XIX of 1957; U.P. Act XV of 1960; U.P. Act III of 1961; U.P. Act XXXIII of 1961; U.P. Act IX of 1962; U.P. Act X of 1965; U.P. Act XX of 1966; U.P, Act VI of 1969; U.P. Act 19 of 1970; U.P, Gaon Panchayat and Kshettra Samitis Act, 1971; U.P. Panchayat Raj (Sanshodhan) Adhiniyam 31 of 1972; U.P. Rural Local Self-Government Law (Amendment) Act 3 of 1973; U.P. Panchayat Raj (Amendment) Act No. 37 of 1976.

(i) The Gaon Sabha

In the hill districts of Kumaun, less than one percent of the villages have a population of 1500 or more.[5] Ninetynine percent of the Gaon Sabhas were, therefore, constituted by grouping two or more villages. Geographical contiguity was the main criterion for effecting such grouping, but Gaon Sabhas were, however, organized *patti, patwari*, circlewise, so that a Gaon Sabha covered only such of the villages as lie in one *patwari* circle. According to the provisions of the Principal Act of 1947, a Gaon Sabha was to cover a larger area and population, which necessitated the composition of Gaon Sabhas by grouping several villages. But the amended Act of 1955 provided for smaller Gaon Sabhas. Thus, in Kumaun Division the position was as follows:

TABLE - 6

COMPOSITION OF GAON SABHAS IN KUMAUN IN 1949[6]

District	Total No. of Gaon Sabhas	Population in 000s	Av.	Area in Sq.m.	Av.	Villages No.	Av.
Almora	773	749	1.0	5495	7.1	5294	7.0
Nainital	256	261	1.0	2729	10.6	1629	7.0

District Almora includes Pithoragarh district and Nainital includes hill, Bhager and Tarai areas.

TABLE - 7

COMPOSITION OF PANCHAYATS IN KUMAUN IN 1956[7]

Sl. No.	Description	Almora	Nainital
1.	Rural population in 000s	749	261
2.	Area in Sq. miles	5495	2721
3.	No. of revenue villages	5294	1629
4.	No. of Gaon Sabhas	2242	545
5.	Average population per Gaon Sabha	334	480
6.	Average area per Gaon Sabha in Sq.m.	2.5	5
7.	Average No. of villages per Gaon Sabha	2.4	3

5. See pp. 33, 34, 35 Tables No. I, II and III above.
6. Cf. : Tewari, G.D : *Rural Self-Government in Kumaun Hills*, Unpublished Ph.D. Thesis from Agra University, 1961, p. 65.
7. Cf. : Ibid, p. 66.

The following table represents the position of Gaon Sabhas in Kumaun in 1979 :

TABLE - 8

POSITION OF GAON SABHAS IN KUMAUN IN 1979[8]

District	Total No. of Gaon Sabhas	Total rural population[9]	Geographical area in Sq. km.	Total No. of revenue villages	Density in Sq. km.
Nainital[10]	676	367199	3533	1788	1595
Almora	1221	649622	5427.746	3159	2680
Pithoragarh	803	369221	8845.350	2272	1789

On 1.4.1956, the total number of Gaon Sabhas constituted in panchayati forest unit villages was 993 (901 in Almora,[11] 92 in Nainital). These Gaon Sabhas are single village units. Majority of the Gaon Sabhas (i.e., 67.7 percent) are multi-village organizations. Only 12 percent of the total number of villages have single village Gaon Sabhas.[12]

(ii) Gaon Panchayat

It is the executive body of the Gaon Sabha. The number of members in addition to the Pradhan, has been fixed according to the population of different Gaon Sabhas.[13] The average number of villages per Gaon Sabha being 2.7, each village has been represented by 6 persons on the average. But the position varies considerably from one Gaon Sabha to another and in respect of different villages comprising the Gaon Sabhas in accordance with their population as indicated below :

8. Figures are compiled from the District Statistics Offices, Nainital, Almora and Pithoragarh.
9. Cenqus Reports of 1971.
10. Figures in respect of Nainital include Bhabar and Tarai areas also.
11. Almora includes District Pithoragarh also.
12. Tewari, G.D. op. cit., p. 66.
13. Rule 3 - of U.P. P.R. Act.

TABLE - 9

DISTRIBUTION OF VILLAGES IN GOAN SABHA IN KUMAUN[14]

District	No. of Gaon Sabhas having villages										Total
	1	2	3	4	5	6	7	8	9	10	
Almora[15]	923	524	325	222	91	58	34	19	16	20	2232
Nainital	142	110	94	65	63	26	25	8	6	6	545
Total	1065	634	419	287	154	84	59	27	22	26	2777
Percentage	38.3	22.8	15.0	10.3	5.5	3.0	2.1	.97	.75	.96	100

There is provision for reservation of seats for scheduled castes, but there are very few panchayats having scheduled castes members in Kumaun hills. The elected members of the Gaon Panchayat co-opt a woman member from amongst the women members of the Gaon Sabha,[16] but in none of the panchayats, under study, women were co-opted.

(iii) Nyaya Panchayats

A Nyaya Panchayat is constituted for a group of about 1 to 10 contiguous Gaon Sabhas. In 1978, in the whole Kumaun Division, 283 Nyaya Panchayats were present.[17] Though the average number of Gaon Sabha and the villages covered by a Nyaya Panchayat circle is 10.5 and 30 respectively, yet individual cases present sharp contrasts. There are some Nyaya Panchayat circles which cover only 6-7 villages, and on the other hand, some of the circles cover as may as 76 to 80 villages.[18]

In determining the area of Nyaya Panchayat circles too, the principle of grouping the Gaon Sabhas of one *patwari* circle in one Nyaya Panchayat, has been followed. The smaller *patwari* circles (i.e. *pattis*) from one Nyaya Panchayat circle, but some bigger ones have two or three Nyaya Panchayats.

Functioning of Panchayats in Kumaun

(i) The Gaon Sabha Meetings

Apart from the two compulsory meetings (i.e. the Kharif and the Ravi meetings)

14. Quoted from Tewari, G.D : op. cit., p. 67.
The figures relate to the position as it was in 1956. But since then some changes have been made in organizing the village panchayats. Cf. Table 8 p. 31.
15. The District Almora includes District Pithoragarh also.
16. Section 12 of U.P. P.R. Act.
17. Nainital - 72, Pithoragarh - 81, Almora 130.
18. Cf. Tewari, G.D : op. cit. p. 73.

per year, the Gaon Sabhas are required to meet informally on the occasions of various important festivals or in specially convened meetings.[19]

Of these two formal and compulsory meetings, the kharif meeting in which the Annual Estimate of Income and Expenditure is to be approved, is convened by all the Gaon Sabhas. But the other one (i.e., the Ravi meeting) in which the reports of the activities of the panchayat are to be considered, is not being held in many of them.[20]

Informal meetings of the village people on special occasions may not be characterized as those of the Gaon Sabhas, but they are generally the folk-assemblies of the people belonging to one or sometimes different villages, and such meetings do take place occasionally when common problems are considered.

Meeting Proceedings

The majority of the members of Gaon Sabhas, are unfamiliar with the rules of procedure to be followed in the conduct of business in the meetings. They do not observe the prescribed formal procedure. The drafting and recording of formal proceedings in the Minute Books is, therefore, done by the Panchayat Secretaries themselves.

Generally, the business is transacted through peaceful deliberations. The attitude of co-operation in proposing and discussing the schemes of village development in the meetings of Gaon Sabhas has been more marked than that of opposing them. The tendency of indulging in heated debates appears to be motivated by personal ends, and the dissenting faction does not offer constructive criticism. A large number of people have been showing such indifference towards the proposals discussed in the meetings of Gaon Sabhas.[21]

More than 60 per cent of the resolutions are moved either by the Panchayat Secretaries or by the Pradhans, some 30 per cent by the members of Gaon Panchayats and the rest by other persons who are the members of Gaon Sabhas only.[22] The resolutions are moved at random as the discussions on particular subjects proceed. As many as 90 per cent of the resolutions are passed unanimously. The necessity of putting them to vote seldom arises, except in case of tax proposals or when a particular group of section of the village community, due to some selfish motive is opposed to a proposal.

The Gaon Sabha assemblies have failed to exhibit that type of interest as is evinced in the informal meetings of the villagers in devising ways and means to

19. Section II (I) of the U.P. - Panchayat Raj Act, 1947.
20. Observations made by us through the sample survey of seven Kshettra samitis in Kumaun Division.
21. These observations are based on personal enquiries made in the seven Kshettra Samitis and the replies received from the survey of 63 village panchayats.
22. Ibid.

solve their socio-economic problems through co-operative consultation and joint effort.

(ii) Gaon Panchayats

Meetings—The Gaon Panchayats in these hill districts have not been able to hold regular monthly meetings. The meetings of Gaon Panchayats are also very poorly attended.[23]

Meeting Proceedings

In most of the Nyaya Panchayat circles different dates of every month have been fixed for different Gaon Panchayats to meet. Formal intimation about the holding of the meetings is not circulated beforehand. Some members often do not remember these dates which are according to the English Calendar. Very few Gaon Panchayats have *panchayat ghars*[24] where the notice about the meetings and agenda could be displayed for the information of the members. Verbal information is generally passed and, in fact, the agenda is rarely prepared beforehand.

Most of the Gaon Panchayats have actually no preconceived business to transact in the meetings. The few resolutions which are occasionally moved in the meetings are recorded in the Minute Book without much deliberation. The responsibility of executing the resolutions passed in the meetings is thrust on the Pradhans or the Panchayat Secretaries alone. Most of the members do not extend whole-hearted co-operation and interest in their execution. More often many a resolution passed in the meetings are confined to their being recorded in the Minute Books only.

Generally Functioning

The Committee system in the functioning of Gaon panchayats as stipulated by the Act, has not been adopted anywhere.

The panchayat executive holds no collective responsibility to the Gaon Sabha. A system of collective responsibility requires a highly developed party system which neither exists nor is desirable in the case of these rural local bodies, for it might lead to unhealthy factions and feuds in the rural society.[25] The Pradhan and the members of Gaon Panchayats do not have the power to check and balance one another. The village assembly (Gaon Sabha) possesses the power to remove the Pradhan, but not the whole executive body through a motion of 'No Confidence'.

The panchayat executive lacks organizational solidarity. Their successful functioning has depended largely upon the personal tactfulness of the Pradhans

23. See Table 34.
24. Nainital - 143, Pithoragarh - 176, Almora - 133.
25. Cf. Tewari, G.D. : op. cit., p. 85.

who are the real executive authority, and their resourcefulness and ability to enlist the desired co-operation from the members of the Gaon Panchayat in particular, and the people in general. Such of the Gaon panchayats as are under the conscientious and sincere Panchayat Secretaries take keener interest in their activities. A large number of Pradhans and the members of panchayats are unable to perform any activity without constant guidance and help from the Panchayat Secretaries in their day-to-day functioning.

The number of Gaon Panchayats in a Nyaya Panchayat circle is too large to enable the Panchayat Secretaries to devote themselves to the activities of all of them effectively and efficiently; sometimes they cannot attend the meetings of the panchayats. This leads to the postponement of the meetings, because the panchayat office bearers do not care to hold them in the absence of the Secretary. More often when the Secretary visits the Gaon Sabha Headquarters, the records are not available to him for their completion, if the Pradhan is absent from the village.

External Control

(i) State Level

The State Government have reserved for themselves certain powers of control over the organization and functioning of the Panchayati Raj, but have delegated some of these powers to the agencies subordinate to them.[26] Thus, at the State Headquarters, the Director of Panchayats, assisted by some Deputy Directors constitutes the main authority to exercise control over the Panchayati Raj administration in the whole State. The Directorate of panchayat functions under the Local Self-Government Department of the Secretariat and the Development Commissioner.

So far as the organization and functioning of the rural local self-government in Kumaun is concerned, the departmental heads at the State level depend upon the information received by them from the subordinate services at the district or village levels about the rural conditions prevailing in these hill areas. Certain aspects of rural administration with which the panchayats are occasionally concerned, viz., question of land management, administration of civil forests, etc. are outside the jurisdiction of the State Directorate of Panchayats.

It is impossible for the Directorate to have a first hand knowledge about the problems of organization and functioning of thousands of panchayat units in different localities of the State. Decentralisation of control on local and regional basis, particularly in respect of Kumaun hills, where rural conditions present

26. Schedule I to the Rules made under the U.P. P.R. Act.

some peculiarities, quite distinct from those in the plains seems essential. With the enforcement of the Kshettra Samitis and Zila Parishad Adhiniyam, wherein control over the village panchayats and their working is exercised by the Kshettra Samitis and the Zila Parishads, the problem seems to have been solved to some extent. Efforts have been on to establish more and more kshettra Samitis areas to serve the rural localities conveniently and effectively.

(ii) The Zila Parishad Level

At the Zila Parishad level, the District Magistrate is responsible for the general supervision of the organization and administration of panchayats in the district.[27] In the discharge of this responsibility, he is assisted by the District Panchayat Officer who is also the District Planning Officer. The day-to-day routine work of the panchayat administration is, however, supervised by the Assistant District Panchayat Officer.

The number of panchayats in each of these hill districts is so large that the District Magistrates cannot be expected to exercise their individual judgement in the discharge of some of their main responsibilities which include the determination of the territorial jurisdiction of the panchayats and constituencies thereof; the nomination of the Panches of Nyaya Panchayats and other office bearers of the Gaon Panchayats against the seats remaining vacant after the election. In these hill districts, the difficulty is more apparent in view of peculiar geographical conditions, large size of the districts and the absence of the means of communication in the interior. The District Magistrates are required to have a tour of the rural areas in the district for three months every year.[28] But it is rather impossible for them to come in close touch with various localities during these tour periods. There is a hierarchy of bureaucratic machinery with the District Magistrate at the top to control panchayat activities and administration. Hence, in actual practice, the District Magistrates simply give their approval to the proposals put before them by their subordinate staff.

The Assistant District Panchayat Officers have to deal with the routine work of thousands of panchayats in the district. They also cannot possible be expected to scrutinize thoroughly the lists of assessments of taxes and the budgets of all the panchayats in the district before giving their approval to them as required by the U.P. Panchayat Raj Act.

(iii) The Field Level

At the field level, different sets of officials have been associated with the panchayat

27. Manual of Government Orders, Para 934.
28. Manual of Government Orders, Paras 249 and 252.

administration. The first category of these officials consists of the sub-Divisional Magistrates (Sub-Divisional Officers or Deputy Collectors), the Tehsildars and the Munsifs; the second one includes all the officials attached to the Development Blocks particularly the Assistant Development Officer (Panchayats) and the third one are the field services belonging to different administrative departments, whose co-operation and guidance is often desired by the village panchayats in carrying on their responsibilities.

The Sub-Divisional Magistrates are required to tour the rural areas in the Sub-Division for one month to six weeks in a year, in which they are required to supervise the work and formation of Gaon Sabhas and the Nyaya Panchayats.[29] They hear petitions in connection with panchayat elections and the revision applications against the judgements of Nyaya Panchayats[30] in criminal cases. In civil cases, such revision applications are heard by the Munsifs.

The need for holding the conferences of the Sarpanchas and the Chairmen of different benches of Nyaya Panchayats in some central localities during the tours of Sub-Divisional Magistrates and the Munsifs has to be stressed.

At the field level, some sort of supervisory control of the Sub-Divisional Magistrate over the activities of panchayats would be more effective, because by virtue of their status as revenue officers and their responsibility to maintain law and order, they still wield sufficient influence in rural areas. Through their proximity to the rural localities they would be able to control the panchayat administration effectively. Since the panchayats are concerned with local self-government and rural development, the association of the block level authorities as expert guides of the panchayats, and empowered to supervise their activities with Sub-Divisional Magistrate's supervisory control over the Block Development Officer, should not be ignored.[31]

The Three Tier Structure of Panchayati Raj Bodies in Kumaun

Kumaun Division has undergone several territorial changes in the past. Uptil 1961, it included the four districts of the entire tract, namely, Almora, Nainital, Garhwal and Tehri. By the year 1961, it was felt that a separate border division should be created. Consequently, a separate Uttarakhand Division lying on the Chinese-Tibetan Frontier, consisting the districts of Pithoragarh, Chamoli and Uttarkashi came into existence. Later for administrative convenience, this whole Hill Division was further divided into two full-fledged Divisions of Kumaun and Garhwal, the former now consists of the districts of Almora, Pithoragarh and Nainital districts. The district of Nainital covers the Bhabar and Tarai areas as

29. Manual of Government Orders, Para 250.
30. Section 89 of the U.P. P.R. Act.
31. Cf. Report of C.O.P.P., Vol. II, Part I, p. 66, Recommendation No. 71.

before.

Pithoragarh district, carved out of Almora district in 1962 was the most backward Tehsil of Almora. The area was totally isolated from outside world. Motorable roads did not exist. Vast distances along difficult terrain had to be traversed on foot. Ponies and goats were used for transportation purposes.

Since the formation of the district in 1962 modest efforts were made to develop the rudimentary infrastructure conducive to agricultural and industrial growth. "Now roads, communication system, electricity, basic agricultural and horticultural facilities together with elementary industrial development facilities have come into existence,[32] though yet quite inadequate for launching a major I.R.D. programmes.

The U.P. Kshettra Samitis and Zila Parishads Adhiniyam, 1961, is the outcome of the recommendations of C.O.P.P.

This legislation was enacted with a view to providing for the establishment of kshettra Samitis and Zila Parishads in the districts of U.P. to undertake certain governmental functions of the block and district levels respectively in furtherance of the principle of democratic decentralization of governmental functions and for ensuring proper municipal government in rural areas, and also to correlate the powers and functions of Gaon Sabhas under the U.P. Panchayat Raj Act, 1947, with kshettra Samitis and Zila Parishads.[33]

Composition of Kshettra Samitis and Zila Parishads in Kumaun

Under this Act, which came in force in Kumaun Division on May 5, 1962[34], the three districts, viz. Nainital, Almora and Pithoragarh of Kumaun Division have been divided into khands or blocks. There is a kshettra Samiti for each khand. In Kumaun Division, the position of these khands or Development Blocks, as at present, is as follows:

TABLE - 10

COMPOSITION OF DEVELOPMENT BLOCKS IN KUMAUN DIVISION IN 1979

Sl. No.	Districts		
	Nainital	Pithoragarh	Almora
1.	Okhalkanda	Kanalichanna	Bhasiachhna
2.	Betalghat	Digttar	Dhauladevi
3.	Ramgarh	Berinag	Hawalbagh
4.	Bhimtal	Dharchula	Lamgarha

32. Project Report, *Hill Area Development Agency*, Pithoragarh, 1977-78, 1981-82 (U.P.)
33. Cf. Preamble to the Act.
34. Section 3 of Kshettra Samitis and Zila Parishads Adhiniyam.

Sl. No.		Districts	
5.	Haldwani	Pithoragarh	Bageshwar
6.	Ramnagar	Gangolihat	Garur
7.	Kashipur	Munakot	Kapkote
8.	Bazpur	Munchari	Takula
9.	Rudrapur	Champawat	Bhikiasen
10.	Khatima	Barakot	Chaukhutia
11.	Gadarpur	Lohaghat	Dwarahat
12.	Dhari (Padampuri)	-	Salt
13.	Sitarganj	-	Syalde
14.	Kotabagh	-	Tarikhet

Functioning of Kshettra Samitis and Zila Parishads

The U.P. Kshettra Samitis and Zila Parishads Adhiniyam provides that every Kshettra Samiti and Zila Parishad must hold meetings at least once in every two months.[35] In these hill districts, it has been noted that special meetings of the members are also convened sometimes.[36] The attendance was generally high. Not a single meeting had to be adjourned for want of quoraum. The Pramukh, or if the Pramukh is absent from the Kshettra, the Senior Up-Pramukh or if the latter is also absent from the Kshettra the Junior Up-Pramukh convenes a meeting of the Kshettra Samiti upon a requisition made in writing by not less than one-fifth of the members of the Samiti[37]. The Adhyaksha or in his absence from the district, the Up-adhyaksha convenes a meeting of Zila Parishad upon a requisition made in writing by not less than one-fifth of the members of Zila Parishad.[38]

In Kumaun Division, except the district of Nainital excluding the Bhaber and Tarai, the other two districts are comparatively very large in size. Due to peculiar geographical conditions the absence of the means of communications and the existence of thinly populated and isolated villages, the interests of all the village communities are not represented in the district level organization.

External Control Over Zila Parishad and Kshettra Samiti

The Government of U.P. had declared[39] the Commissioner of the Division as the 'prescribed authority' for all the Zila Parishads and Kshettra Samitis within the Division to exercise the powers of general supervision. Likewise, a Mukhya Vitta

35. Section 82(2) and Section 61(2) or Kshettra Samitis and Zila Parishads Adhiniyam.
36. Study of seven sample Kshettra Samitis meetings.
37. Section 84(2) of K.S. and Z.P. Adhiniyam.
38. Section 61(2) of K.S. and Z.P. Adhiniyam.
39. Section 225(1), Notification No. 691-A/XXXIII-7-R-1961, dated February 18, 1963.

Adhikari (Chief Finance Officer) Zila Parishad has been appointed in each district to exercise the powers relating to all matters affecting finance and accounts of the Zila Parishad or the Kshettra Samitis in the district.[40]

The State Government has the power to remove the member of the Zila Parishad.[41] The Commissioner of the Division has the power to remove a member of the Kshettra Samiti[42] on the same grounds on which the State Government is empowered to remove a member of the Zila Parishad under Section 231 of the Act.

In exercise of the powers conferred on him by the Act, the Governor of U.P. has framed the U.P. Zila Parishad Rules, 1963.[43] Under these Rules, the Adhyaksha exercises the control over the Mukhya Adhikari and other heads of departments of the Zila Parishad.[44] The Mukhya Adhikari have administrative control over all officers and servants employed with the Parishad, except the Vitta Adhikari. The Parishad has the general control over the Vitta Adhikari.[45]

Each Kshettra Samiti has a Khand Vikas Adhikari.[46] The Pramukh of the Kshettra Samiti has a general control over the Khand Vikas Adhikari and all other officers and servants employed with the Kshettra Samiti work under the general control of the Khand Vikas Adhikari.

The laws, rules and notifications governing the administration of the Panchayati Raj are framed on same uniform lines for the whole State. Due to peculiar conditions, difficulty has to be faced in their proper application in these hill districts of Kumaun Division. There is lack of actual contact between the State Level authorities exercising control over panchayat administration and the rural local bodies in Kumaun. The secondary source of information of the State level authorities cannot convey to them the real position of these typical hill localities. The district and field level officials have to carry out the orders and instructions issued by the State level authorities. Local responsibility and initiative cannot develop su :h conditions.

40. Section 225(2), Notification No. F133-A/XXXIII-7-R-1962, dated August 8, 1963.
41. Section 231 of Kshettra Samitis and Zila Parishads Adhiniyam.
42. Section 236(2) of Kshettra Samitis and Zila Parishads Adhiniyam.
43. Section 51 Published with Government Notification No. 1502-B/XXXIII-9-R-63, dated December 10, 1963.
44. Section 45 of the Act. There shall be Chunao Samiti consisting of the Adhyaksha (Chairman), a member of the Karya Samiti and a Secretary.
45. Section 51 of Kshettra Samitis and Zila Parishads Adhiniyam.
46. Section 49(1) of Kshettra Samitis and Zila Parishads Adhiniyam.

3

PLANNING FOR RURAL DEVELOPMENT

The term planning has been indiscriminately used in economic literature and any type of governmental activity, having a definite goal has been taken to mean as planning.[1] Indian Planning Commission opines that the term "Planning evolves the acceptance of a clearly defined system of objectives in terms of which to frame overall policies. It also evolves the formulation of a strategy for promoting the self realization of the ends defined. Planning is essentially an attempt at working out a rational solution of problems, an attempt to co-ordinate means and ends, it is, thus, different from the traditional hit and miss methods by which 'reforms' and 'reconstructions' are often undertaken."[2]

In fact, major assumption which makes democratic planning real is confidence in the community that the national plan aims at achieving a social order in which economic disparities will be greatly reduced and equal opportunity afforded to all; that no privilege, no interest is sought to be sustained, even for a period, except in the degree in which it fulfills a larger social purpose. This can furnish the ingredients of social cohesion within the community.[3] How seriously the states themselves took their responsibilities for 'planning from below' is not easy to say. Uttar Pradesh, for instance, after classifying the various state programmes according to levels of operational responsibility and sources of finance, attempted to specify in some detail the planning duties of officials, from the District Officer to the V.L.W., and of representative bodies, from the Zila Parishad to the panchayat.[4]

Plans Relating to Social Welfare

The concept of welfare state is dynamic. "A nation is judged from the status accorded to its women and children. It becomes important, therefore, that the less fortunate women and children living in the villages receive opportunities for relishable growth and development so that they are able to pull their weight in the national endeavour for establishment of a better social order based on liberty, freedom and equality."[5]

1. Tandon, B.C : *Economic Planning : Principles and Problems*, Allahabad, Cahitanya Publishing House, 1963, p. 1
2. Govt. of India : *The First Five-Year Plan*, Planning Commission, Delhi, 1952, pp. 7-8.
3. Ibid, p. 144.
4. Uttar Pradesh, *Third Five-Year Plan* : Report, pp. 2-3.
5. Desai, Morarji. : *Social Welfare*, Vol. XXV No. 5-6, New Delhi, C.S.W.B.

The field of social welfare work is, therefore, difficult but challenging. The results achieved are seldom spectacular. The beneficiaries of welfare schemes should be those who start with severe handicaps, broken homes, untimely deaths, economic hardships, natural disasters, social inequalities, etc. In the field of social welfare, new problems keep emerging everyday and one has to take cognizance of these problems. There is need for preventive services more than curative programmes now. In relieving the people of their sufferings, what is required more than funds, is dedication and spirit of mission.

The concept of social welfare and its policies have undergone a big change in the past decade. The traditional concept of welfare state was characterized by humanitarian attitude directed towards groups, with special problems. Today there is a growing awareness to gear the social development approach to the removal of poverty and to render service to the rural population, and more so to the socially and economically backward groups including women, children and the handicapped persons. There is greater stress on integrated development. In this comprehensive sense, social welfare policies encompass social services, social security measures, community services, labour welfare programmes and services and nutritional programms and services, all under one ambit. In this process of gradual but perceptible change over, social welfare has become institutionalized, since we speak of welfare of more deprived sections of population, i.e. children's welfare, women's welfare, welfare of the handicapped, welfare of the aged, etc. Social welfare services are provided to improve social status of all individuals particularly of those belonging to backward, weaker and vulnerable sections of the society.

Social welfare as an integral part of overall national development has found its momentous place in our Constitution[6] which lays down various Directive Principles of State Policy and imposes a duty upon the State Government to follow them in making laws. All these directives point to the establishment of a welfare state. The Constitution affirms that "the State shall strive to promote the welfare of the people by securing and protecting as effectively as it may provide, a social order in which justice, social, economic and political shall inform all the institutions of the national life."[7] The other provisions in the Constitution[8] relevant to social welfare are the directives relating to economic equality, welfare of women and children, free and compulsory primary education, general civil code, prohibitory promotion of weaker sections of society, etc.

To translate into action, the above provision of the Constitution, and to meet

6. *India's Constitution*, Article 37.
7. *India's Constitution*, Article 38.
8. Chapter IV of the Constitution enumerates these provisions in various Articles (Art 39 to 51).

its basic objectives, a programme of economic and social development came to be included in the Nation's Five Year Plans. A number of planned social welfare activities have been initiated since then for the uplift of socially and physically handicapped people and for women and children, and other weaker sections of the community. The Five Year Plans rightly stress a variety of social services, programmes of education, health and family welfare, housing, welfare of the backward classes and the like, which are mainly directed towards achieving the national objectives of social justice.

There are quite a few urgent problems facing social welfare sector, which need immediate attention, such as elimination of destitution within a specific period, protection of children against exploitation, raising the level of nutrition of children, better diet for expectant and nursing mothers, gradual introduction of prohibition, improving the status of women, and the like. In order to achieve these objectives, strenuous and sustained efforts are needed with increased financial allocations and activity for social welfare, specially in remote backward areas like Kumaun Hills, because they have some peculiar geographical and economic features.

In the new approach, there is emphasis on the integration of welfare and developmental services. Efforts are also being made to integrate social and economic planning programmes for weaker and vulnerable sections. Welfare services are promoted with family as a unit of development and are integrated with programmes of employment, economic development and distributive duties.[9] Simultaneously, efforts are also being made for the provision of basic health services, such as maternity care, family planning, functional literacy, child care and other social services to families in general, and to those of weaker and vulnerable sections in particular.

There is need for non-official organizations to effectively function at all levels -state, district, block and village. They should be allowed to work with dignity, responsibility and partnership so as to take the form of a nationwide movement. In a democratic set-up, government will have to rely more on peoples' participation in the planning and implementation of rural developmental programmes and the more so, in the programmes relating to social welfare. To perform their role effectively greater representation and encouragement has to be given to such voluntary organizations and they have to be considered as equal partners in the task of national reconstruction. Their deep involvement can pay rich dividends as they enjoy many advantages over the official machinery. At the same time, if voluntary organizations are to assume greater responsibility for social welfare

9. One such scheme is "Food For Work" programme undertaken by various State Governments in recent years.

schemes, it is necessary that they conduct their work on scientific and systematic lines, and have access to specialists and experts for necessary advice and guidance.

It has been felt that there is a great need for publicity of the programme to be brought home to such village/block/district level voluntary organizations. Many of the voluntary agencies are perhaps not fully aware of the socio-economic development programmes, and are not in a position to grasp the advantages of these schemes. The local bodies like Panchayats and Zila Parishads could be motivated about the objectives of the programmes and the benefits which could be derived by the weaker sections of the community. Their help could be sought in the formulation of district level committee which would go a long way in meeting the situation.

Till recently, social welfare planning was confined to providing curative and rehabilitative services, but now there has been a shift in the approach and efforts are underway to integrate social and economic planning programmes for the weaker sections of the rural areas. Welfare cannot be fragmented or compartmentalized. It should be taken in its totality and it should be integrated with the institutions and requirements for rural development. It includes within its fold all social services. In rural areas, we have yet another problem, namely, the provision of services for those affected by social disability such as untouchability, widowhood, destitution as well as dependency arising out of the loss of earning of the bread-earner due to crime, drunkenness, etc.

Though many new policies and programmes have been adopted by the Union and State Governments for promoting social welfare, yet the results achieved so far may not be regarded as satisfactory. There is still too much to be achieved.

Education

The greatest asset of a nation is its people, and no national goal is more significant than the release of their potentialities—for individual growth, for productive work, and for enlightened citizenship. Human development is the key to all other development. And the essential ingredient of human development is education."[10] The pre-requisite for the success of rural democracy is to awaken civic consciousness among the masses through a planned organization of social education. "The ultimate overall objective of social education should be to give people the vision of a new order and enthuse them with a new determination to bring it about.[11] The programme of social education should aim at acquainting people with the

10. Bayard, H. Price. (Edited) : *Rural Reconstruction and Development*, New York, Frederick A. Praeger, Publishers, 1967, p. 201.
11. Cf. Report of U.P. Evaluation Committee, 1959, p.18

fundamentals of citizenship and the way democracy functions, inducing them to learn how to read and write, imparting them training for refinement of emotions and instilling a spirit of toleration among them."[12] The programmes of social education as planned and executed by the Assistant Development Officer (Social Education) in the Community Development Block areas in U.P. did not meet with success in achieving these objects. Hence this office had to be reorganized.

Another object of programme of social education is the training of the village leadership. The Pradhans and Sarpanchs of village panchayats need to undergo a training course at the Block or Panchayat Samiti level soon after the elections and before these functionaries are allowed to hold office. A well planned course of instruction needs to be framed. It should include training in the maintenance of accounts and other important records, procedures of holding the meetings and the conduct of business in them, methods of planning development projects, knowledge and implication of panchayat laws and rules, etc. In U.P. some such arrangements were made during the Second Five-Year Plan period. But they did not evoke the desired response and as such did not prove effective. An effective revival of these is very necessary.

The aim of social education must, therefore, be to give to the illiterate adult, the minimum knowledge required for a purposeful civic life. It recognizes the right of every individual to develop the resources of mind and improve upon his heritage. Social education, besides promoting literacy, aims at education for citizenship and democracy and the fostering of social solidarity and cultural harmony in the country. It brings among the adults an awareness of their rights and duties, and develops in them the love for a democratic way of life and pride in their cultural heritage.

Social education also implies training in the basic principles of personal and social hygiene. If people know how diseases are caused and how to fight them, hundreds of valuable lives can be saved from premature and untimely deaths, besides improvement in the general health of the people. By emphasizing sanitation, balanced diet and nutrition among the masses, it is possible to build a healthy nation. It is implied in the process of social education that the education of the individual in terms of his personal and social hygiene is a responsibility towards society.

It is equally necessary to satisfy the emotional and aesthetic needs of adult learners. Painting, music, dramatic performances, festivals, exhibition and melas can be profitably used for the development of aesthetic sense towards cultural activities in the adults, besides enabling them to demonstrate their creative powers and organizational ability. Group activities and discussion, talks, sports,

12. Cf. Report of C.O.P.P. Vol.I, para 16.2, p. 154.

clubs, educational, cultural and historical tours, youth camps, seminars and gardening have also been found valuable for a social education programme.

The opportunity to improve one's economic condition is one of the prime attractions of education. Hence, a programme of social education has to initiate the adult into ways and means of raising his living standard. The social education worker should, therefore, associate himself with the organizations which can teach the individual improved methods of agriculture or new crafts that can add to his earning capacity.

Finally, social education stands for human brotherhood and universal ethics. It teaches the virtues of peace, and is opposed to narrowness of outlook in any form, such as chauvinism, casteism and racialism. It upholds the dignity of man and attempts the elimination of poverty and backwardness.

Children cannot be left out of a programme of social education. As social education is a continuous process, beginning from birth, the school and the playgrounds. It plays an important role in promoting social education among children. Experience shows that participation by children, youths and adults in groups and community organizations is the best method of social education. Through group participation individuals find opportunities to work with others, to express their creativeness, to develop their ability and to qualify for leadership depending on their ability to perform a given function. In addition, group participation also promotes a spirit of cooperation and brotherhood.

Social education, as a process of education for life in society, has an extremely vital role to play in community development by relating villagers with their own community and their social groups. This should be in harmony with the current emphasis on the organization of three vital institutions, namely, the panchayat, the cooperative and the school. Through the programme of social education, various voluntary organizations such as youth clubs, farmers' associations, women's clubs, recreation and cultural groups act as agencies for associating the villagers with the community development programme and providing a base for developing leadership.

Therefore, the Social Education Organizer, who is to be a member of the team of Development Officers, must try to promote organizations of the groups described above. Every extension worker should act as an educator in his own subject, and every social group, including the panchayat and the cooperative, should offer the opportunity to promote social education among the members of the community. Thus social education would become an integral part of the total programme of Community Development in rural areas.

Health

Health is a gift of life to which man has a right. Late Pandit Jawaharlal Nehru emphasized the need for special attention to village health and for extention of the benefits of health to the entire countryside.

The primary care is educative in matters of health as well as of economy. Health is closely connected with wealth. Investigations have to be made to find out what the villages can be supplied in the shape of drugs. Amongst the stocked medicines, a few like castor oil, quinine, tincture of iodine, soda and boiling water, etc. are at present the most common medical agents. The most effective way of relief from diseases is to attend to sanitation. The practice of "The Nature Cure" should be adopted, as it does not require high academic qualifications or much erudition. Simplicity is the essence of Universe, observance of the rules of personal, domestic and public sanitation should be imbibed to eliminate most of the diseases. Gandhiji rightly claimed, "I hold that where the rules of personal, domestic and public sanitation are strictly observed and the care is taken in the matter of diet and exercise, there should be no occasion for illness or disease. Where there is absolute purity, inner and outer, illness becomes impossible. If the village people could understand this, they would not need doctors, Hakims or Vaidyas."[13]

Lack of good nutrition is basic to all health problems in rural areas. It is hoped that through emphasis on educational methods, which stress the importance of better nutrition, it may be possible to lay a solid foundation for popular and steady efforts to improve nutrition. The scope and quality of care, however, are still very limited. There are hardly and lady doctors in rural areas. Almost all rural births are attended only by a midwife, trained or untrained, and the number of trained midwives falls far short of even the minimum needs.

Life means something more than mere physical survival. Apathy concerning life is a greater tragedy than apathy concerning disease and death, and apathy concerning life will be dispelled only by overall economic and social development, not merely by health measures. Much about healthful living can be learned, and will be learned, when general education becomes universal and when millions of people are no longer condemned by poverty to live not only in ignorance but in squalor. India's overall attack on the causes of poverty, on environmental sanitation, on health education, and on family planning will in the longrun yield greater results in general, physical and social wellbeing than curative medicines.

---

13. Gandhi, M.K : *Rebuilding Our Villages*, p. 20.

Economic Activities

"The need for comprehensive planning based on a careful appraisal of resources and on an objective analysis of all the relevant economic factors has become imperative. These purposes can best be achieved through an organization free from the burden of the day-to-day administration, but in constant touch with the Government at the highest level."[14] After Independence, India launched a nation-wide programme for rural awakening and faster social change, so as to facilitate a 'total change' in the economy. It is widely recognized that "development is not a mechanical process of adding to capital stock, human skills, technological knowledge and artifices, but a matter of institutional change of attitudes and behaviour patterns of all those intangible elements that distinguish a human society from a field of particles or a çolony of ants."[15]

The main thrust of the Union Government's economic policy is towards removal of poverty and creation of employment opportunities through accelerated economic development of the rural sector, with special emphasis on agricultural production, cottage industries, small industries and arts and crafts. "To a very large extent economic development is a cumulative programme of self-improvement on the part of communities. If given some encouragement and reinforcement from the outside, most people can do much better with the meagre resources available to them than they have done in the past. If, in addition, they are continuously provided with useful items of information, they can improve themselves still more."[16] In any meaningful scheme for rural development, it is imperative that economic and social life of the rural poor should be improved by providing subsidiary occupation to them.

Agriculture is, of course, a crucial factor in the economic growth of the rural sector in India. The experience of the past, however, indicates that increase in agricultural productivity alone does not solve the problem of rural poverty. On the contrary, it has increased the gap between the rich cultivators and the poor farmers and landless labourers, resulting in acute discontent among the large majority of rural population. This side effect of the "green revolution" can be corrected by helping the small and marginal farmers in improving their agricultural operation. Creating minor irrigation facilities, motivating the small and marginal farmers to adopt improved methods of agriculture, increasing credit facilities for the purchase of agricultural equipment, etc. are some of the areas which need immediate attention for the success of an I.R.D. programme.

---

14. No. 1-P (C) 50, Gazette of India, 15 Mar, 1950.
15. Krishnaswami, K.S. : "Some Thoughts on a Drama" *Finance and Development*, I.M.F. Washington, Vol. I, 1969, p. 45.
16. Meier Richard, L. : *Development Planning*, New York, McGraw Hill Book Company, 1965, p. 331.

Increased investment in agriculture can raise productivity but it does not ensure a corresponding increase in employment. Therefore, investment syndrome need not dilute our enthusiasm for developing programmes that could create more and more subsidiary occupations for our small farmers. For example, the potential of forestry in generating employment is much greater than any other sector in most parts of the country's rural area, specially in hill areas. It is also significant to note that substantial forest employment is located in remote and backward areas where other employment opportunities are generally non-existent.

Agro-based industries have also a great potential for providing supplementary part-time employment to farmers and their families, e.g. processing of rice, cotton ginning, preparation of milk and milk products, oil extraction, jute manufacture, etc. The setting-up of cottage and rural industries will also help to stop the tendency of migration to cities.

Economic and social life of the rural poor consisting of small and marginal farmers, landless labours, tenants and other weaker sections, can be improved by providing subsidiary vocations to them. The task of rasing the standard of living of the rural poor can be accomplished either by increasing productivity directly from land or through subsidiary occupations to the vast multitude of the rural people to enable them also to participate in the overall developmental process. Such a programme requires promotion of not only agricultural and allied activities but all other dimensions of rural economy like mining, forestry, road construction, communication, cottage and rural industries, etc.

Agriculture

The question of stepping up agricultural production in a larger context, is linked up with a number of basic issues. These are: strengthening of the administrative machinery of the Agriculture Departments of the State Governments, achieving better coordination between the Union Ministries concerned, active involvement of the panchayati raj institutions in the programme of delegation or decentralization of adequate powers to field officers and panchayats with a clearer definition of the administrative and technical roles of individuals and institutions, streamlining the supplyline and imparting a sense of direction to the programme. Irrespective of these problems, however, a beginning has to be made at the base, viz. at the village level to prepare the village or the panchayat agricultural production plans, as the only means of involving cultivators in the village in the agricultural efforts and mobilizing effectively the resources of the local community to this end.

In the context of the national emergency and the urgent need for increasing agricultural production, it is necessary that the scope of agricultural production plans should be limited to a few selected items based essentially on the fuller utilization of local resources. In other words, so far as agricultural production is concerned, the Community Development Programme has to be reorientated with a view to intensify such efforts for increasing agricultural production as are likely to yield quick results.

The preparation and implementation of such a plan should primarily be the responsibility of the Village Panchayats and the Panchayat Samitis, who should carry out this responsibility in collaboration with the cooperative societies and other voluntary organizations. It is expected that associate organizations like Youth Clubs, Mahila Samajas, Farmer's Forums, Village Volunteer Force, etc. should be involved in the process as far as possible. All these bodies will, of course, be guided and assisted in their efforts by the higher agencies, both official and non-official, viz. Panchayat Samiti, District Central Co-operative Societies, the District Agricultural Officer, the Collector, the Zila Parishad, etc.

The production plan has necessarily to be a simple plan so that it is understood by all who are involved in the programme. It should be unencumbered with complicated and voluminous proforma. The scope of the plan should be restricted by involving a selected number of progressive agriculturists in each village within the jurisdiction of the V.L.W. The Plan should also directly emphasize and aim at a positive increase in the production of principal crops in the respective areas, rather than the mere adoption of improved agricultural practices. The plan has to be based on achievements and definite targets for increasing production by a reasonable and agreed quantity. Such targets should then be split up and assigned to individual agriculturists, according to their capacity, enthusiasm and willingness to adopt improved agricultural methods. Such an approach to the preparation and execution of the plan would create a psychological atmosphere for its successful working. It would also create among the participants a sense of contributing their mite to the national effort and increasing agricultural production as a second line of defence and would provide a motive force to the individual agriculturists for adopting improved agricultural practices as a means to achieve this goal. It is necessary to relate plans more explicitly to the panchayati raj bodies in order to enable them to play their part in enthusing the village community into action.

In view of this 'target-based approach' to the subject, the method of preparation and the content of the plan has to be as follows :

1. There should be only one plan for the entire area covered by a panchayat instead of separate plans for each revenue village. Such a plan should be more conveniently called a 'Panchayat Agricultural Production Plan'.
2. Such plans should be drawn up by every Panchayat with the assistance of Village Level Workers and in consultation with the village co-operatives. For the immediate present, the plan could be prepared and implemented for at least one major food crop and one major commercial crop having the highest

acreage under each in the area of the particular panchayat. In areas where are more than one major crop of each category, plans may be prepared for two food crops and two commercial crops.

3. In respect of each crop, the panchayat should set definite targets for increasing production in the panchayat area by a reasonable and agreed level arrived at on the basis of voluntary undertakings given by individual cultivators and institutions in respect of their holdings within the area of the panchayat.
4. Targets of increased production can be planned to be achieved through the use of a limited number of recommended practices which will constitute the minimum agricultural programme. More particularly, the programme can, for the present, comprise the following :
   a) Development of local manure resources including (i) compost, (ii) farm yard manure, and (iii) annual and perennial green manure by individuals and institutions.
   b) Use of recommended and improved varieties of seeds and seed treatment.
   c) Adoption of dry farming practices comprising (i) cultivation across the slope, i.e. contour bounding; (ii) strip cropping; (iii) repeated harrowing and frequent inter-cultivation; and (iv) wider spacing and thinner sowing.
   d) Adoption of plant protection measures, both preventive and curative, on a collective basis.
   e) Fuller and better utilization of available irrigation facilities where water is made available up to the field boundary; and
   f) Double cropping, whenever feasible.

Minor Irrigation

Agriculture needs assured water supply in order to be more productive. It is only irrigation that makes a cultivator free to choose his crops and the rotation in which they should be grown. It keeps the fields busy throughout the year and provides employment to members of farming family and their bullocks.

Irrigation is the most acutely felt need of the farmers, they want a more regular flow of water where canals exist. A programme of agricultural engineering must, therefore, lay adequate stress on providing a regular and reliable supply of irrigation water.

Horticulture

The horticulture enterprise has a very important role to play in the rural economic development plans. Though orcharding would generally be undertaken by big farmers who have consolidated pieces of land and also the ability to invest capital, yet the development of fruit industry is essential. It has employment potential for small farmers, marginal farmers and landless labourers. The U.P. State Government has provided enough progency orchards, nurseries and plant protection teams, etc. for developing orchards. By strengthening the existing governmental facilities horticultural development could be boosted.

Nursery

The supply of good quality seed and seedlings is the most important factor for successful cultivation of fruits and vegetables. The development of nursery for the supply of vegetable seeds and fruit seedlings deserves maximum attention. Since vegetable seed production is a highly specialized job, it strengthens the vegetable seed production farm at various places.

Provision for Water Tanks

During summer months water is not available even for drinking and other domestic purposes. The most critical period when too much scarcity of water is felt is from the middle of April to the middle of June and this period is the most important for vegetable production. Water storage tanks must be constructed on the important areas which may give a boost to the vegetable and fruit growers and also an incentive for other farmers.

Rejuvenation of Old Orchards

There are two ways for increasing fruit production: first, by establishing new orchards; and second, by improving the productivity of existing orchards. Extention of area under orchards cannot be done indefinitely. Therefore, increasing the productivity of existing orchards is very important. The existing orchards are more or less like nurseries for many diseases. Development of these orchards requires pruning, training, replacing the plants and spraying and dusting of the diseased plants.

Requirements of Fertilizers and Pesticides

Besides the control of various diseases and pests, use of fertilizers in orchards also needs encouragement. Correctly dosing of fertilizers has been carried on considerably but intensive efforts are needed to apprise each and every cultivator of correct dosage in accordance with the requirements of crops and soil. The people exhibited reluctance to the extensive use of chemical fertilizers because they are afraid and rightly so, of its long-range effects. They, on the other hand, preferred green manuring and natural compost. In view of the prime importance of compost in raising horticultural production, this programme needs to be undertaken on a campaign basis.

Transport Requirement

In order to have speedy and timely work quick transport is a must. It is important for three reasons; (a) seedlings of vegetables and fruits must be supplied to the farmers in time. (b) Technical persons, whether of the agricultural universities or State Government, must reach the individual orchards as and when required and (c) the produce being highly perishable, should be transported from the orchards to the market in time.

Cold Storage

It has been seen that because of the lack of proper storage facilities at the terminal, or consuming market, fruits worth lakhs of rupees are wasted so many times. It is, therefore, suggested that the construction of cold storages at important marketing towns and cities should be undertaken in order to give better prices to the orchard planters.

Marketing

Marketing is one of the most important factors effecting the development of area and also improving the economic condition of farmers. In the case of fruits and vegetables, the marketing is done either of the fresh or of the processed product. As mentioned earlier, quick and easily available transport facilities must be made available for this purpose. Another important factor in marketing of fruits and vegetables is fine packing. The packing cases used for packing of fruits like apple, peach, plum, etc. are very costly. So, there is a need to make available the packing cases, baskets, etc. to these farmers at reasonable prices.

Finance

The vegetable growers and orchard planters always bank upon external agencies for availability of money for the purchase of materials. Therefore, credit facilities must be provided to the farmers at reasonable rate of interest.

Cottage Industries

From the outset, the aim of the rural industries programme has been to increase the earning capacity and self-respect of rural families by creating or expanding cottage type, money-earning industries that could be operated with minimum capital, using locally available raw materials."[17] The rural industries programme is considered to be the weakest programme in the Community Development.

17. Bayard, H. Price. (Edited) : op. cit. p. 178.

This, despite the fact that the need for concerting the present purely agricultural economy into an agro-industrial economy, has imparted urgency to this programme. No doubt, a series of measures have been adopted to put the programme on an even scale, but the progress made so far has not been commensurate with the efforts put in. The odds are, no doubt, heavy against rural industrialization, but the want of a clear-cut policy decision at the top level and the paucity of men and material in implementing the programme at the bottom, are largely responsible for its slow progress. The introduction of Panchayati Raj on a countrywide scale, and the consequential involvement of the people in planning and execution of development programmes have acted as morale booster and given hope for a brighter future in this field. It would be wrong to presume that the programme did not receive due attention in the past. Rather, it was agitating the minds of our planners shortly after the C.D. programme was ushered in.

Under the Panchayati Raj Organization, the Block or the Kshettra Samiti level has become the main unit of planning and administration of development programmes and apparently it is directly responsible for the implementation of the schemes of rural industries also. All these measures have had the desired effect, and rural industrialization received the much needed impetus. The initiative of Panchayati Raj bodies in the matter lends vitality to the programme and all States in the country have started in right earnest the implementation of the programme.

Training of artisans, creating a cadre of skilled workers to meet the needs of a developing rural economy and financing artisans to set themselves up in their trades are the practical needs of the programme. As a result of development activities, the repairing and servicing of oil engines, welding, etc. and the manufacture of improved agricultural implements have become new items of work in the rural areas. The existing skills, therefore, have to be improved and new skills have to be introduced in the villages. In order to meet the situation, the State Khadi Board, has provided short term training facilities in some training centres set up by it in the villages. The Industries Department is also imparting training through its Industrial Training Institutes. The Block Training Centres, however, have not proved effective in introducing improved practices and the 'response ratio' of the artisans to the training has also not been very impressive.

Gandhiji visualized the fact that "agriculture today, on account of many factors like small holdings, its sub-division and fragmentation, etc. is not a paying preposition." Evil practices of the village money-lenders, and exploitation by them of villagers add salt to injury. That is why the salvation of Indian villages lies in the revival of village cottage industries, thereby also creating self-employment. "Though articles may be manufactured by villagers in their cottages, they can be pooled together and profits divided. The villagers may work under supervision and according to plan. The raw material may be supplied from common stock. If the will to cooperative effort is created, there is surely ample opportunity for cooperation, division of labour, savings of time and efficiency of work."[18] The articles which the villagers manufacture may be crude, but they can be improved by improving their workmanship. The articles manufactured in villages must not be dismissed just because they are not produced in big cities or factories and are not of superior quality. In other words, the artistic talent of the villagers should be evoked. Gandhiji rightly declared, "We are guilty of a grievous wrong against the villagers, and the only way in which we can expiate it, is by encouraging them to revive their lost industries and arts by assuring them of a ready market. If we neglect our duty to our villages, we shall be courting our own ruin. This duty is no onerous one. It is incredibly simple. We have to be rural-minded and think of our necessities and the necessities of our household in terms of rural mindedness. The task does not involve much expenditure either. It is in consonance with the true economics of our country."[19]

Even a cursory examination of the exsiting situation reveals that the integrated rural development programme have been lost sight of in its actual implementation. The Industries Departments and the State Khadi Boards have not broken down the plan for the development of rural industries and the funds are not channelized through the Block administration. By and large, the Block is not being treated as the unit of planning and implementation as suggested by C.O.P.P. Since the State Khadi Board is in charge of the programme, the Industries Department has lost touch with the Block agency. This has created a situation in which the Block is concerned only with the promotion of village industries and the Khadi industry is being looked after by the Department of Khadi, through its own officers. There is, thus, no effort to co-ordinate the activities of different departments working for the same object at the Block level.

Another problem that needs to be examined is whether various Development Departments may be expected to organize and actively participate in rural industries programme, or their role be only to assist, guide and supervise the work done in the Blocks. Viewed from any angle, the rural industries programme in India has yet to live up to the hopes once held for it and has yet to make significant headway. The pre-conditions for the successful introduction of modern technology into rural industries do not yet exist in India; and until there are sufficiently widespread electrification, basic overheads, technical skills and the like, the planners will be much handicapped.

18. Gandhi, M.K. : *Rebuilding Our Villages*, p. 31
19. Ibid, p. 37.

Co-operatives

"In India, as in many other countries, co-operation started as a means of ensuring for the poorly equipped citizens advantages which better placed persons were able to command by their own individual resources. The principle of mutual aid, which is the basis of co-operative organizations, and the practice of thrift and self-help which sustain it, generate a sturdy feeling of self-reliance which is of basic importance in a democratic way of life. By pooling their experience and knowledge and by helping one another, members of co-operative societies can not only find the solutions of individual problems but also become better citizens."[20] The principle of co-operative society is" all work for each, and each works for all."[21]

The co-operative movement has been in existence in the country for about sixty years; yet the movement has not lived up to the expectations of its founders. Numerous causes which need hardly any repetition have been reported by various committees, commissions, economists and specialized academicians for the failure of this socio-economic movement. The non-official wing of the movement, however, always contends that the movement has largely failed on account of the rigid official control. The soul of this movement according to them has been 'suffocated' by the stifling interference of the officials. In their opinion, co-operative movement should be free from Government control and as such, they deprecate the dependence of cooperative movement on officialdom.

The co-operative movement, as is well-known, is based on the concept of mutual help and self-help. Nobody should, therefore, ordinarily dispute the claims of the non-official co-operators that the co-operative movement is a people's movement and managed by the people for themselves. But the paradox is: who is there to prevent the spontaneous growth of the un-official character of this people's movement? The State and the officials come to the scene only because the movement was not developing on its own initiative. It is a well-known fact that ever since the Co-operative Credit Societies Act of the Govt. of India came in force the movement had the moral, material, and financial support of the Government. Excessive bureaucratic control is, no doubt, to be deprecated but to allege that all the ills of the movement are due to excessive governmental control over it, is far from the truth. Without the State support and patronage, there would probably have been no trace of the movement worth the name. Even if this State support was to go today, the movement in many parts of the country would collapse like a house of cards.

20. Government of India : *First Five Year Plan*, Planning Commission, Delhi, 1952.
21. Arthur F., Raper. : *Rural Development in Action*, Cornell University Press, Ithaca and London, 1970, p. 285.

Shri S.K. Dey (Former Union Minister of C.D., Cooperation and P.R.) has rightly observed: "The Cooperative movement, with notable exceptions, had grown to be the preserve of many vested interests. All types of people from saint to the villain had rushed into co-operative movement. Control co-operative organization from the ground to the national level continues to be vested with notable exceptions, in a narrow circle which cannot be dislodged, however hard one may try. There are outstanding examples of services. But alas, the instances of exploitation are far too many in comparison. What is worse, the needy rarely get the help meant for them."[22]

In the past, many parts of India were indeed fortunate in having the services of selfless and zealous non-officials who devoted every ounce of their energy to propagate the mission of co-operation without caring for honours or honoraria. It is a lamentable yet true fact that the co-operative movement has largely failed to attract men of integrity and missionary zeal to catch the imagination of the people. To get the services of persons who are prepared to dedicate themselves to the cause of this socio-economic movement is a real problem in many parts of the country. So long as there is dearth of such devoted and selfless non-officials, there is no escape from reliance on official control and supervision.

All our thinking now is based on the panchayat and the village co-operative and giving them power and authority to take decisions, and also to make mistakes, as they might. The solution to the shortcomings of the co-operative movement in most of the rural areas lies not in the hasty de-officialization as has been suggested by some non-official cooperators, but in simplifying the rules and procedures, avoiding red-tapism, inefficiency and slackness on the one had and eliminating unfair dealings and vested interests on the other.

The villagers and peasants can make the best use of their available resources through cooperation. In fact, cooperation is the basis of the entire Community Development programme whose aim of socio-economic uplift can be achieved only through cooperative efforts. Integrated Rural Development can be put on a sound foundation only when there is a network of cooperative farms, service cooperative societies and other such cooperatives.

Activities Relating to Local Self-Government

Gandhiji once observed, "self-government means continuous effort to independence of government control, whether it is foreign government or national. Swaraj-government will be a sorry affair if people look up to it for the regulation of every

22. Quoted in, "De-Officialisation of Cooperative Movement", by B.S. Mathur, *Kurukshetra*, Vol. 15. 1965.

detail or life."[23] Reconstruction of rural local self-government in the post-Independence period owed a great deal to the demands made in the Five-Year Plans for popular co-operation in the execution of schemes for the development of agriculture, animal husbandary, cottage industries, etc. The Five-Year Plans, therefore, placed special emphasis on the role of local bodies in the field of development and they took the view that, "The Constitution has provided for democratic institutions at the centre and in the States, but so long as local self-governing institutions are not conceived as parts of the same organic constitutional and administrative framework, the structure of democratic government will remain incomplete."[24] The plans, therefore, made out a case for reorganizing local bodies in rural areas from both the economic and political standpoints.

Village self-government is known to be as ancient in India as the community life itself is. Municipal governments flourished in ancient and medieval India at quite a later stage, while the panchayati form of self-government was widely prevalent right from the Vedic age in rural India. Within the feudal or semi-feudal structures prevalent in those days, local government offered a stable basis of organized life at the local level. Liberal ideas that had grown with modern education created an appreciation of the importance and need for local self-government.

The present structure of rural local self-government has been fashioned anew to meet the needs of economic development and it may be said to be a co-partner of the community development launched in 1952. It is the result of an effort to translate into institutional terms the nationalist political ideas of village autonomy and democracy.

Local self-government in India as at present may be classified into two main groups, viz. (i) the rural local self-government or the system of panchayati raj institutions and (ii) the urban local self-government. The panchayati raj covers the entire rural population and consists of a three tier structure of popular institutions from the village to the district, formed on democratic principle and having an organical link. In pursuance of the Balwantrai Mehta Committee Report on democratic decentralization (1957), the panchayati raj institutions have been entrusted with various powers of local government including developmental functions pertaining to rural localities in their respective jurisdictions.

"Democratic theory, with its distinctly sharp accent on the needs, interests and susceptibilities of the citizen, imparted by transforming local government into local self-government, a new dimension and justification to the former. The period during which this took place, spanning the evolution of the modern

23. *Young India*, 6 August, 1925.
24. Venkatarangaiya, M. and Pattabhiram, M. (Edited) : op. cit., 1969, p. 254.

industrial civilization, witnessed expansion in the activities of local self-government. To the traditional function—watch and ward, charities, repairs to roads, bridges and churches, were added 'civic' functions—protected water supply, drainage, street cleaning and lighting, regulation of markets and traffic, and sanitation and health in general. Later, local public works and educational facilities joined the array; democrats also visulaized local self-government as an arena of political education, and a nursery of representative government."[25] These are sturdy roots indeed. The case for local self-government in the context of modern democratic civilization can be summed up as follows: It increases the efficiency of the political system as a whole by reducing the scope for abuse of power and costly mistakes incidental to excessive centralization. It serves as a feedback mechanism, a mechanism which is self-corrective in some respects so far as the provision of services to citizens in the proximate environment is concerned. Services in which citizens are in general more interested tend to judge the performance of a democratic government as a whole. Only local self-government would be in a better position to appreciate the environmental uniqueness of localities and their problems, needs, styles and perceptions.

The traditional civic welfare and regulatory functions are associated with local self-government. A glance at the categories of functions performed by the local self-governing bodies would make the point clearer. The major functions of these bodies may be grouped as follows:

1. *Gaon Panchayat*

Sanitation and health; public works; agriculture; forests, animal husbandry; village industries; welfare activities and promotion of voluntary bodies; education; sports and culture and general administration and security.

2. *Kshettra Samiti*

Sanitation and health; public works; planning; coordination; supervision and execution of developmental programmes including agency functions.

3. *Zila Parishad*

Public works; planning; coordination; supervision and execution of developmental programmes including agency functions.

In fact, civic welfare and developmental functions cannot be classified too neatly; they are bands in a spectrum. The traditional functions—civic welfare and regulatory—figure prominently only at gaon panchayat level; planning,

25. Shiviah : "Centralisation and Panchayati Raj : A Developmental Perspective." *The Indian Journal of Public Administration*. Vol. XXIV No. 3, 1978 p. 681.

implementation and coordination of developmental programmes loom large at higher levels. Most present developmental services, e.g. education, hospitals, public works, irrigation, animal husbandry, etc. are divided between the field units of the State Government and the new local authorities. The control of local authorities is greater, however, where civic amenities are concerned. Devolution of powers has not so far endowed local authorities with complete control of any service. The dual system of local administration, one under the field agencies of the State Government and the other under the new local authorities, which has been a distinctive feature of the local self-government in India since its inception, remains.

Civic Amenities

Sanitation, conservancy, public health, street lighting, safe drinking water supply, maintenance of village roads, culverts, schools, etc. come under civic amenities. Other functions which are optional, include setting up and maintenance of library, reading room, community hall, playground and recreation facilities, maternity and child welfare centres, cart and bus stands, burial ground, etc. As regards development work, the panchayats generally function as agents of the Samitis or Zila Parishads. The Panchayat Samities or the Kshettra Samities, as they are designated in U.P., took over the development functions performed earlier by the Community Development Block. Besides, they have also to perform civic functions such as the administration of primary education, health and sanitation, including rural dispensaries, and maintenance of village roads and minor irrigation works.

If we decide to reconstruct the villages and go to them, our duty would be to reach self-help and we will then find the glory of the villages. In the words of Gandhiji, "Men or women who would go to the villages would tell the village people that it would be their duty to keep their village clean and make them self-supporting. They must not expect the Swaraj Government to do these things for them. Our villages are on the verge of destruction owing to the disappearance of village industries. They can be revived only by a revival of village industries. Among these industries, the spinning wheel occupies the centre. The others easily arrange themselves around the wheel. Thus everybody will learn the value of industry, and if all will engage in industries conductive to the welfare of the State, several lakhs of rupees will be saved, for the people by the people. And it can be shown that by putting into practice the ideal of self-help and self-sufficiency they will have to pay the lowest taxes and realize a greater degree of happiness in the sun than is possible under any other system."[26] Thus, it is the duty and privilege

26. Gandhi, M.K : *Rebuilding Our Village*, pp. 4-5.

of village panchayats to represent the community in all matters affecting village polity and economy.

Community Development Plans

Community development is a movement designed to promote better living for the whole community with the active participation and the initiative of the community. Community Development has been described as a "process of change from the traditional way of living of rural communities to progressive ways of living; as a method by which people can be assisted to develop themselves on their own capacity and resources, as a programme for accomplishing certain activities in fields concerning the welfare of the rural people; and as a movement for progress with a certain ideological content."[27] The objective is promotion of the all round development of the rural communities, economic, social and cultural. Hoiberg[28] defines community planning in a similar way by saying it is "the systematic application of forethought to problems, of C.D." Thus, C.D. can be described as the efforts of the community to identify its problems and to attempt to establish and reach its goals.[29]

As a concept of growth and consistent with democracy both in developed and developing countries, the community development plan has already come to stay. It has acquired global position. As the concept has grown in India, community development demands for its fulfilment support from three major pillars. One of the pillars is what has come to be known as Panchayati Raj. The second pillar is Sahakari Samaj (Cooperative Society). The third pillar is the chain of associate institutions based entirely on voluntary effort of individuals gathered together for common purposes.

Community Development may thus be defined as a process in which people unite and pool their resources in an effort to improve economic, social and cultural conditions of the community. It is a programme of developing material and human resources to the fullest extent and in a co-operative manner. Community Development is a movement, designed to promote better living for the whole community with the active participation and initiative of the members of the community itself. "In matters of rural development, it emphasized the importance of building up an infra-structure (e.g. irrigation, anti-erosion, and land—reclamation measures), point to need for popular participation through co-operative societies

27. Mukerji, B. : *Community Development in India*, New Delhi, Orient Longmans Limited, 1967, p. 2.
28. Otto G. Hoiberg, : *Exploring the Small Community*, Lincoln, University of Nebraska Press, 1955, p. 12.
29. Kreitlow, Aiton and Torrence. : *Leadership for Action in Rural Communities*, Inc. Danville, Illinois, The Interstate Printers and Publishers, 1965, p. 10.

and panchayats, and anticipated the 'block' system which was subsequently to provide the administrative foundation of the Community Development Programme."[30]

The effectiveness of the village panchayat, its strength and its vitality depend upon the sustained, intelligent, and enthusiastic interest and co-operation of the village community in its affairs and activities. The village should become a larger unit not only economically but also politically. The panchayat should be an effective self-governing body, completely independent in the sphere of activities entrusted to it. Then only, it can perform economic functions envisaged in I.R.D. programme. The village panchayats could be made viable to function as a self-governing unit by encouraging its members to tap local resources by way of providing matching contribution to the Government grants. The task that the villages face can never be tackled unless there is united and collective effort. A community spirit must be created before there could be proper community development. It would be the duty and privilege of village panchayats to represent the community in all matters affecting village polity and economy. They would be the main local agency for execution of various programmes of the Government affecting vitally the welfare of villagers, and would represent the Government in all activities in the village. They must have control over village sites and other communal property.

Besides these representative functions, they can also perform regulatory functions such as supervision of elementary schools and encouraging sports and other extra-curricular activities in them, looking after the village dispensary and maternity and child welfare centres, ensuring non-pollution of drinking water, removal of encroachments, and keeping roads clean. Lastly, they may perform such service functions as rural welfare work and promotion of cultural activities.

Problems there are and will be in plenty but there is also wide determination to resolve them. Much evaluation goes on and the anger in the present situation is that too much may be expected too quickly before the systems have settled down. By that time, say ten years hence, we shall know whether the system has succeeded. If it does not, then the results will be grave indeed for development plans, and with them democratic methods of fulfilment will have been found wanting. Basically, however, the system is sound and the will to make it work is widespread.

30. U.P., *Industries Reorg. Committee, Report* (1934), p. 9.

Rural Development Through Three Tier Organization

In order to make grassroots democracy effective and to ensure the maximum degree of people's participation in the implementation of the community development programme, C.O.P.P. recommended the three tier structure of local bodies in the district. At the base, primary unit was to be the village panchayat, the Panchayat Samiti was to occupy the intermediate position and the Zila Parishad replacing the old district boards was to be at the apex. The Study Team laid down in details the principles which should guide the constitution of these three tier bodies, the devolution of power and financial resources for these units and their relationships to one another. It made its recommendations sufficiently flexible as regards the details for the implementation of this scheme of democratic decentralization which the State Governments could work out through suitable enactments according to varying conditions obtaining in them. One of the basic feature of the recommendation of the study team was that it not only emphasized people's participation in implementing the community development schemes, but it also suggested a close association of the official machinery at all the three tiers with the people's representative bodies.[31]

The institutions of panchayati raj, i.e. the village panchayats, Samitis and Zila Parishads are primarily local governments at their respective levels, and secondarily the agencies of the State Government. To treat the Panchayati Raj as a programme, unconnected with anything bigger or higher or more comprehensive will have no driving force. Gandhiji had said, "That Government was the best that governed the least;" but today we are moving in the contrary direction. In the name of Socialism and Welfare State, the government, which means a centralized bureaucratic machinery, is taking upon itself more and more functions and the people's minds are being corrupted so that the elite in this country are demanding that everything must be done by the government. Gandhiji's philosophy was "that people should be free from all sorts of state intervention; the restraints should be from within; they should be disciplined from within. Likewise, he was committed to the establishment of a Welfare State. But it is feared that we might, in the name of creating a Welfare State, get a system in which the individual will lose his identity, in which there will be no freedom and the human spirit will be crushed. Whereas the aim should be as Gandhiji observed, "that the whole of society should become as much like the family as possible. Beyond the family is community, beyond that wider and wider association of communities of human beings, the world community."

Not much could be done if the entire local sector development is planned and implemented from the state capitals. "Democratic planning presupposes an overall

31. C.O.P.P. Vol. I, Chapter II.

unity of policy combined with proper diffusion of power and responsibility. In such planning, not only the Governments of States but also local self-governing bodies, such as municipalities, district and taluka boards and panchayats, and various functional organizations have to play a vital part. Measures to promote a healthy growth of such institutions, are, therefore, an integral part of democratic planning...In the implementation of plan, again, the principle of diffusion of power and responsibility must be followed."[32] But once the three tier structure of Panchayati Raj is introduced and adequate resources and staff transferred to them statutorily, the effects are bound to be much more concrete. What is more, a local leadership has emerged, which as it gathers more experience and training, is able to put these transferred resources and authority to better and more effective use in the interest of the community, being close to the field and to the problems faced by the people. In short, as Dr. Iqbal Narain has observed: "the decision-making process gets accelerated. Mistakes in taking decisions in implementing them are also detected and taken cognizance of much earlier and corrective steps taken simultaneously." All these are the happy by products of decentralization. Whatever may be the criticism or inadequacies of Panchayati Raj, nobody will venture to suggest returning to the old days when everything was planned and implemented by departmental bureaucracy from the State capital.

To conclude, it must be remembered that rural development through three-tier organization is not an end in itself, it is only a technique or a method. Its success depends on a careful and uniform planning of policies at higher levels and a conscious commitment of devolution of power and responsibility to the lower level organizations with minimum interference from above, adequate transfer of staff and resources and a constant dialogue within the organization and careful monitoring. The whole idea is that it is not a rigid formula but a continuous process of give and take, of finding out the shortfalls and loopholes, plugging them effectively, using the most important resources, viz. the man in the organization whose decision-making skill has to be perfected to show results.

Such re-examination is not a need of Indian democracy alone. The institutions of every democratic society require constant debate of their underlying principles in order to remain democratically alive. Institutions of local self-government everywhere are in special need of re-examination today, as the services required by local communities become increasingly complicated.

32. Hanson, A.H., op. cit., 1966, pp. 90-92.

4

PLANNING AND EXECUTION OF RURAL DEVELOPMENT PROGRAMMES IN KUMAUN

Planning and Execution of Rural Development Plans

Nothing was more definitely stated in the First Five-Year Plan and more universally accepted than the purpose to strengthen and use the village panchayats as the units of action in the rural development programmes. The aim is that in each individual village, people should work out their own plans for the solution of their socio-economic problems. In all sectors of development, rural areas demand the highest priority. The greatest need of the hour is the revival of rural based programmes to be implemented with greater emphasis on the development of typically backward areas like the hill districts of Kumaon and Garhwal in U.P. about which it may be said that these communities lay much behind in integrating welfare services with development. We have to touch the problems of rural folk at the grassroots. The most important single problem in rural reconstruction and agricultural extension is the evolution of an integrated pattern of welfare organization.

Agriculture

In the hilly areas of Kumaon Division about 90 per cent of the net cultivated area is rainfed and modern intensive methods of crop production cannot possibly be applied in these hilly districts. Besides, there are problems of progressively deteriorating land base because of lack of appropriate soil and water conservation measures, small and scattered land holdings, lack of high yielding crop production, technology suited to the hill environment, and lack of institutional framework to support agricultural methods.

Land Holdings

Although the total per capita land available in the hill area is higher than that in the plains, yet a major part of the total area here is forested and rocky. Consequently, per capita arable land is very small. The position in the hill districts of Kumaon is indicated by the following table:

TABLE - 11

DISTRIBUTION OF AREA INTO HOLDING[1] AND NON-HOLDING CATEGORIES IN KUMAUN HILLS[2]

Districts	Cultivated Area Hectares	Non-Culti vated area Hectares	Total Area Hectares	Percentage of A to C
	A	B	C	
Almora	84323	399607	483930	17.4
Pithoragarh	59332	199424	258756	22.9
Nainital	25573	45983	71056	36.0
Total Kumaun	169228	644514	813742	20.8

These figures indicate that the total area under cultivation in Kumaun hills is about one fifth of total area. As a result, per capita land is very meagre in the hills, i.e. about 2 per acre. There is no consolidation of land holdings which is impracticable here and even if proposed would be highly resented because such a scheme could not possibly be implemented judiciously. Consequently every individual farmer's land holdings are scattered here and there.

Irrigation

The region is endowed with ever covered snow peaks which give water throughout the year through many rivers and streams. The main rivers flowing through these areas are Kosi (Almora, Nainital) Ramganga (east and west), Gomti (Almora) Nandhaur, Pindar, Sarju, Panar, Gola, Kamin, Dhauli, Ladhia, Kali, etc. Besides, there are many lakes particularly in the district of Nainital, namely, Nainital, Bhimtal, Khurpatal, Nal-damyantital, Naukuchiatal. But in spite of these big water resources, the rivers and lakes have practically no utility for irrigation purposes. Village sites on ridges at a high altitude can get irrigation facilities only if water could be channelled through *gools* from rivers, which is practically impossible in majority of the cases. However, in areas which lie in the valleys, the streams are of some help for irrigation there. But in most cases the river valleys are stood deep and steep and the village sites on either side cannot get such facility from them. These resources could present a good potentiality in the

1. Holding area excludes government or village community land. Non-holding area excludes reserved forests and cadastrally unsurveyed areas.
2. Agricultural Census, 1970-71, U.P., p. 79.

irrigational development of the region only by means of a network of canals and pumps or by constructing dams. But it would be a very costly affair and as such an impossibility. Consequently, the water of these rivers is hardly of any utility for irrigation purposes in these hill areas. The lakes mentioned above, too are hardly of any use for irrigation purpose, because in dry months there is no over-flowing from them and their water level goes too deep down.

In spite of considerable attempts made by the Geogical Survey of India, the Central Water and Power Commission and various other research agencies, the agricultural areas in Kumaun remain untouched and unexplored for irrigation purposes.[3] A large number of villages have no water near by even for drinking purposes. Thus, these hilly areas present the lowest percentage of irrigated area to total arable area as compared to other parts of the State. For example, in Western Uttar Pradesh 40 per cent of the land was found irrigable,[4] whereas in Kumaun this is only 7.5 per cent and that too in low lying broad river valleys only.

In spite of these major drawbacks irrigation in hills is practised by *gools* where possible. It is an indigenous method. It is a method of carrying water from the streams flowing through upland ridges to the terraced fields situated on the ridges. These can at the most irrigate very small patches and that too only seasonally. Canals as a modern method of irrigation are almost nominal in Kumaun. At present, the total length of such canals is only about 635 km in the whole of Kumaun hills, excluding the Bhabhar and Tarai areas of Nainital district where they are available to some extent. The number of canals and their length in different districts of Kumaun division is given below:

TABLE - 12

NUMBER OF CANALS AND THEIR LENGTH IN VARIOUS DISTRICTS OF KUMAUN HILLS[5]

District	No. of Canals	Total length (in km)
Almora	97	341
Pithoragarh	50	134
Nainital (Hills only)	58	160
Total Kumaun	205	635

3. Naithani, R.C. : *Water Resources of Kumaun*, Unpublished Doctoral Dissertation, Agra University, Agra, 1971, p. 11.
4. N.C.A.E.R. : *Techno-Economic Survey of U.P.*, N.C.A.E.R., Delhi, 1965, p. 96.
5. Quoted from Pandey, P.C. : *A Study of Changes in Economic Conditions of Scheduled Caste in Kumaun since Independence*, Unpublished Ph.D. thesis from Agra University, 1978, p. 116.

The sources of water for irrigational purpose in these hill villages are minor irrigational channels which are known as *gools*. The number of canals being constructed is less in number and most of them remain dry due to lack of water supply. Irrigation in hills by private sources is mostly by *gools* which is an indigenous system.

The following table shows the area under irrigation in the various districts of Kumaun:

TABLE - 13

DEVELOPMENT OF IRRIGATION BY PUBLIC SOURCES IN VARIOUS DISTRICTS OF KUMAUN[6]

District	Period		
	Before First Plan	Upto Second Plan	Upto 1974-75
Almora	0.0	6.6	7.71
Pithoragarh	0.0	0.0	0.90
Nainital	13.1	89.4	131.80
Total Kumaun	13.1	96.9	140.41

The figures show that only 7.5 per cent of the agricultural land in the region is under irrigation; therefore, by and large, the area is characterized by rainfed agriculture. As the major proportion or rainfall is received during the monsoon season extending from June to September, Kharif is not only the main crop season but also the more productive one. Rabi crops grown in the area have to depend chiefly on sporadic rains. In the valleys where the level of soil moisture in the rabi season is rel: tively better as compared to the hill slopes, productivity is marginally more; broadly speaking, the level of crop productivity is lower in the rabi season than in the kharif.

There is thus an urgent need for extension of irrigation facilities in the districts of Kumaun hills. Not that lack of water resources comes in the way of irrigation development but the problem arises because of the general nature of topography which leads to uneven distribution of water after rains. This hampers the construction of storage reservoirs and canal networks. Added to this, is the problem of high cost of construction and maintenance of irrigation systems in these hills.

6. Ibid., p. 117. In this table the data in respect of Nainital district includes Bhabar and Tarai areas. The position of hill tracts in this district presents the same position as in other two districts.

Cropping Pattern

Cropping pattern in these hill districts differs with soil, climate, irrigation facilities and such other factors, from one area to another. It differs also from that in the plains. The most important cereal crops in the hills in terms of area, output and value are wheat, paddy and *mandua*.[7] The districtwise details of the various crops are presented below:

TABLE - 14

DISTRIBUTION OF THE AREA SOWN UNDER VARIOUS PRINCIPAL CEREALS AS PERCENTAGE OF TOTAL CROPPED AREA IN VARIOUS DISTRICTS OF KUMAUN[8]

Districts	Paddy	Wheat	*Mandua*	Others
Almora	24.7%	35.4%	22.5%	17.4%
Pithoragarh	29.6%	34.2%	22.9%	13.3%
Nainital (Hills)	25.8%	29.8%	2.4%	42.0%

The figures show that more than one third of the total cultivated area is covered by wheat crops. The second largest area is covered by paddy crops in Almora and Pithoragarh districts while in Nainital district wheat comes first. The area under *mandua* is quite insignificant in Nainital district. It is only 2.4 per cent of the total area. The reason is that the crop is not grown in Bhabar and Tarai areas of Nainital district, which constitute the major part of cultivable area in this district. Other crops include gram, maize, potato, barley, vegetables and some minor cereals, pulses, etc. and sugarcane.

Crop Rotation

Rotation of crops is the best way of keeping up the fertility of the soil. Different crops remove different constituents from the soil in various ratios. If we sow the same crop in the same land every year, a larger percentage of certain constituents and less of others will be continually removed and the yield will suffer. Therefore, the pattern of crop is changed every year, so that when one rotation is over, nearly the same percentage in different constituents is removed and this change in crop, in turn, is called crop rotation.[9]

In the hill areas of Kumaun the farmers practise their own technique in this regard, which is also conditioned by the availability of irrigation resources. Due

7. *Mandua* is a coarse grain like *Bazra* in the plains. It is used to make bread and is a food of the poor.
8. Agricultural Census 1970-71, U.P. p. 89.
9. Khushalani, K.B : *Irrigation (Practise and Design)* Vol. I & III, Poona, Allied Book Stall, 1962, p. 36.

to diversity of soil, irrigational resources and the climate, crop rotation in these hills is quite different from that in the plains. In hill areas, the entire land is divided into two parts during the kharif crop. The one part is for paddy and the other for *mandua*. The former includes only paddy and the latter which is sown mixedly with various pulses, like *gauhat* (*dolicus bilorus*), *bhatt*, (a variety of soyabeans or *glycilus vulgar* is), *urad*, *chua*, (*amaranthus frumentaseous*), *johangora* (*oplismens frumentaceous*) etc., is sown in the first fortnight of June and harvested during October and November. Thereafter, the land is allowed to remain fallow, so that it may be used to sow paddy in the month of March.

The extent of continuity on land depends primarily upon the fertility of the land. Even there are such lands where hardly one crop is produced in a year. It is a well known fact in hill areas that higher the altitude, the longer is the span to re-cultivate and vice versa.

Yield and Disposal

It is very strange that in spite of nearly 81 per cent cultivators in the total working population, the hill area is deficit in food grains and has to depend upon imports. There are many reasons for this poor yield in hill areas. Firstly, the area is rocky and soil lacks humidity. Secondly, there is a considerable lack of irrigation facilities and adequate rainfall in the hills. Thirdly, the terraced fields generally ravage during the rainy season and the potentiality of the land flows out of the fields each year. Finally, crops are generally destroyed by hails or drought, every year.

Average yield per acre of principal crops in Kumaun (hills) has been calculated as shown below:

TABLE - 15

AVERAGE YIELD PER ACRE OF PRINCIPAL CROPS IN KUMAUN (HILLS)[10]

Figure in Quintals

Name of Crop	Almora[11]	Nainital[11]
Rice	1210	1210
Wheat	947	874
Barley	806	829
Maize	403	650
Sugarcane	16800	N.A.
Potato	3089	3248
Tobacco	291	291

10. N.C.A.E.R. : *Techno-Economic Survey of U.P.*, 1974, p. 246.
11. District Almora includes District Pithoragarh as well and the position of District Nainital may be taken to mean the inclusion of Bhabar and Tarai area.

The economy of the rural hill districts is predominantly agricultural in character. The hilly areas have been lagging behind in the race of agricultural development. Since about 88 per cent of the net cultivated area is rainfed, there is lack of high yielding crop in this area.

Average yield per hectare of some crops in the year 1973-74 of districts Almora, Pithoragarh and Nainital (Hills) is shown below:

TABLE - 16

DISTRICTWISE PER HECTARE YIELD OF SOME CROPS IN 1973-74[12]

Figure in Quintals

District	Paddy	Maize	*Mandua*	Wheat
Almora	9.9	10.7	11.1	9.4
Pithoragarh	9.0	11.1	11.0	10.0
Nainital (Hills)	9.5	13.4	11.2	10.4

From the point of view of food grains, this hill region, as a whole is a deficit area. A large part of the total holdings is quite un-economical in this hill region. Therefore, the lion's share of the output is consumed by the cultivators. A good number of cultivators are always deficit in food grains every year. Very few of the cultivators are in a position to sell their surplus produce to local consumers only.

The most important economic activity of the Kumaun Division which supplements the agriculture sector directly is animal husbandry. The role of Veterinary Hospitals in improving the breeds or curbing the diseases is quite negligible. The hospitals are situated generally at the Block headquarters and thus, it is very difficult to bring a diseased animal from remote places. However, it should be kept in view that government has opened various hospitals and other institutions. The following table shows the information in this regard:

In Kumaun (Hills) Division the level of agricultural development has been extremely unsatisfactory. The area, does not produce enough foodgrains to meet local demand in full. The need to assign urgent priority to the rapid improvement in agriculture in this area cannot be over-emphasized.

The extremely low proportion of area under agriculture is no doubt attributed primarily to the mountainous terrain of the region. The general topography has other consequences for agricultural backwardness in the region besides the one noted above. There is, for instance, greater incidence of soil erosion. The quick

12. Figure have been collected from the Office of Deputy Director (Agriculture) Kumaun Division, Nainital, 1973-74.

TABLE - 17

VETERINARY HOSPITALS AND OTHER ANIMAL SERVICE CENTRES IN VARIOUS DISTRICTS OF KUMAUN[13]

Particulars	District			Total
	Almora	Pithoragarh	Nainital	Kumaun
Veterinary Hospitals	17	12	29	58
Stockman Centre	51	54	142	247
Sheep farms	2	2	N.A.	4
Sheep-wool-Extension Centres	8	11	-	19
Artificial Insemination Centres	26	2	20	48
A.I.S. Centres	52	N.A.	92	144
Deep frozen Centres	N.A.	35	65	100

run-off of rain water which causes soil erosion also does not allow permeation of water into the soil. Above all, non-availability of water for irrigation and of sub-soil moisture is a general problem of agriculture except in the valleys.

The general topography of the region also has a bearing on the size of land holdings, the extent of fragmentation and the nature of agricultural activity. Because of the steep slopes, fields are generally small strips of terraced land. Apart from leading to unavoidable fragmentation and its concomitant disadvantages this also leads to high cost of land development.[14] Thus, the unfavourable effect of topography on the agriculture of the Kumaun Division are—high risk, low porductivity, and high cost of land development and maintenance.

Problems of Agricultural Development

In the analysis of the prevailing level of agricultural development in the districts presented in the previous section, the extremely unsatisfactory state of affairs is forcefully brought out. The two most important problems of a physical nature which hamper agricultural development in the area are soil erosion and inadequate irrigation facilities. As was briefly noted earlier, the heavy rainfall experienced in the higher altitudes causes considerable damage to agricultural land; land slides and soil erosion are common hazards. Although fields may be terraced, but as due regard for the gradient of land is not given the incidence of soil erosion is not completely eliminated. The extremely poor extent of irrigation development has already been noted. "Among the other factors which hamper agricultural

13. Compiled from the Office of the Deputy Director (Livestock), Kumaun Division, Nainital.
14. Waheeduddin Khan, Tripathy, R.N. : *Plan for I.R.D. in Pauri Garhwal*, National Institute of Community Development, Hyderabad, Avon Printing Works, 1976, p. 30

development in the districts mention may be made of the relatively high pressure of population on agricultural land. At the same time cultivators are not in a position to effect savings out of their meagre income which further disables them in undertaking land improvement and in adopting improved agricultural practices."[15]

Thus, the chief problems of agricultural development of the Kumaun Division, may be attributed to unfavourable land—man ratio, inadequacy of irrigation facilities and soil erosion. However, self-sufficiency in food production alone is not adequate to ensure the future economic well-being of the area as that does not agument the household incomes substantially. The constraints of topographical, climatic and soil factors on the development of agriculture in the area are such that future possibilities of a break-through in crop production are relatively circumscribed. Hence diversification of the agricultural economic base size of holdings, production of field crops alone will not be an adequate base from the point of view of a satisfactory level of income of farm households even if future yield levels are twice high as the prevailing ones. This factor also underlines the importance of supplementary agricultural occupations. Among the lucrative land-based activities to supplement incomes of farm households from field crop production, horticulture and animal husbandry merit special attention. Other land-based activities to support the agricultural economy of the area as a whole is forestry.

Horticulture

The rugged topography of the region does not pose as serious a problem for the development of horticulture as it does for the development of field crops. In fact, hill slopes which cannot be utilized for raising food crops can be used for the development of orchards. Planting of fruit—trees on such slopes is doubly beneficent—as a source of income and as an effective measure to check soil erosion.

Kumaun Division is endowed with the best soil and climatic conditions for growing temperate, sub-tropical and tropical fruits. Apple, pear, peach, plum, apricot, cherry, walnut, almond are temperate fruits, grown between the heights of 4000 ft. to 8000 ft. above sea level. Fruits like citrus, mango, papaya, banana, etc. are sub-tropical and tropical fruits. These fruits are grown in areas having the height between 1000 to 4000 ft. above sea leavel. There are certain spots which have shown a remarkable progress in this direction. The important among them are Ramgarh, Mukteshwar and Paharpani in district Nainital. Lamgara, Kausani,

15. Waheeduddin Khan, Tripathy, R.N : *Plan for I.R.D. in Pauri Garhwal,* National Institute of Community Development, Hyderabad, Avon Printing Works, 1976, p. 37.

Chaubatia, Daunagiri, Shitalakhet and Bageshwar in district Almora and Munsiari, Champawat, Bin, Lohaghat, Kanalichhina, Digtar, etc. in district Pithoragarh.

The following table shows the remarkable progress in the context of horticulture in Kumaun since 1951.

TABLE - 18

DISTRICTWISE AREA AND PRODUCTION OF FRUITS IN KUMAUN DIVISION[16]

District	Area under Horticulture (in Hectare)		Total Production	
	Upto 1951	Upto 1976	Upto 1951	Upto 1976
Almora	800	) 18346	800	) 9228
		)		)
Pithoragarh	-	) 8604	-	) 120
Nainital	1000	20286	1200	60186
Total	1800	47236	2000	81456

The table itself explains that the area under horticulture has increased by more than 26 times, in Kumaun as a whole within a period of 25 years. Total production too has likewise increased by about 40 times in the same period. The following table shows the districtwise production of some important fruits in Kumaun Division in the year 1976.

TABLE - 19

DISTRICTWISE PRODUCTION OF DIFFERENT FRUITS IN KUMAUN DIVISION[17]

Figures in M. Tonnes

Fruits	Districts			
	Almora	Pithoragarh	Nainital	Total
Apple	2157	3641	30709	36507
Pear	1575	1285	1258	4112
Peach	736	475	6442	7653
Plum	1022	1186	3125	5568

16. Figures have been collected from the Office of the Deputy Director (Horticulture), Kumaun Division, Nainital.
17. Holding area excludes government or village community land. Non-holding area excludes reserved forests and cadastrally unsurveyed areas.

Mango	2038	1245	2285	5568
Citrus	1085	2148	1998	5231
Other Fruits	615	2062	4375	7052
Total	9228	12042	50186	71456

In the case of vegetables, the records from the Horticulture Department show that before 1951, the total production of vegetables was only 900 metric tonnes but now the production has increased to more than 3800 metric tonnes during 1978. It is particularly commendable in the case of potato. Earlier than 1951, the production of potato was quite negligible and confined to few selected localities, but by 1978, the production has reached the stage of 11600 metric tonnes, and has attracted many areas to produce this crop.

Problems of Horticulture Development

Horticulture is capital intensive activity involving different operations each with its own peculiar difficulty or problem. Planting of orchards and their maintenance till the trees come to fruition is a stage involving high investment inputs without any returns. Once the tree start bearing fruit, the operations involved are harvesting and pre-marketing processing, storage and packing, transportation and marketing. Some of these operations have a high risk factor while some others are specialized and cannot be efficiently performed by the growers individually. Because of these features fruit growing is a high risk proposition.

Availability of credit for development of orchards and their maintenance is a serious problem in the Kumaun Division. The initial investment required for land development, planting of trees and other necessary works is in most cases beyond the capacity of the local farm households. The gestation period of 5 to 7 years in the case of most fruit trees is too long and unproductive; indeed this is viewed by the farm households as entailing a direct cost, namely the loss of food crops which could have been raised on land. Another important problem is the lack of proper guidance and technical know-how. Although there is a satisfying natural support yet due to lack of resources, receptivity of modern horticulture techniques and absence of properly organized processing and marketing facilities, much progress could not be achieved.

Forestry

Forest can be regarded as the most extensive primary natural resource of the Kumaun Division. Of the total geographical area about 48 per cent is accounted for by forests.

From the point of view of legal status, functions and exploitation, the forests of the area can be divided into three categories. First, the government owned forests in respect of which conservation and utilization policies are decided by the Forest Department, which are called Reserve Forests. Second, forests which are owned by individual villages or groups of villages, and in whose respect utilization polices are decided by the villagers themselves, which are called Community Forests. Third, Private Forests, that is, forests owned by individuals enjoying ownership rights.

The region primarily exports raw materials for paper mills, railway line - sleepers, magnesite, terpentine, resin, wood for carpentry and fuel purposes, woollen-clothes, apple, metal pots, coal herbs, etc. The lion's share of the exports is covered by forest product, which can be evidenced by the following table :

TABLE - 20

STATEMENT SHOWING SOME MAIN EXPORTS FROM KUMAUN FOR THE YEAR 1972-73[18]

Figure in .000 Quintals

Product	To (Place)	Quantity
Wood for match-box	Bareilly	45.3
Medical Plants (herbs)	Lucknow, Calcutta, etc.	5.2
Khair	Bombay	94.6
Ordinary Pine wood	Meerut, Rampur, Moradabad	156.73
Pine wood (Fuel)	Bombay, Rampur, Moradabad	814.20
Wooden Coal	Bombay	33.1
Grass for the use of Paper	Saharanpur	71.6
Bamboo	Kanpur, Delhi, etc.	65.2
Terpentine and Jhula	Bareilly, Moradabad	176.1
Stone, Gravel and Sand	Aligarh, Bhojipura	319.0

From the brief discussion in the preceding paragraph, it is seen that as far as forest products are concerned not only does the region have a potential market, but also has already established substantial commercial links. The demand for timber, bamboo and other forest products of commercial value is likely to remain steady if not increase.

18. Chandra, H : *Problems and Prospects of Road Transport Development in Hill Areas of U.P. with Special Reference to Kumaun Region*, Ph.D. Dissertation, Kumaun University, Nainital, 1976, p. 14.

Problems of Forest Development

While the prospects are indeed not depressing, there are many problems afflicting the forestry sector of the districts. Unauthorized grazing in the forest and lopping of trees is one of the chief problems. Consequently, not only has the forest cover been obliterated but loss of valuable soil cover has also occurred on an extensive scale. The practice of unauthorized grazing and lopping of trees has to be checked effectively in order to improve the performance of the forestry sector.

Apart from the above, the conventional practice of leasing out forests to contractors without adequate supervision and control of the forest department has also been instrumental in aggravating the problem of mismanagement of forest.

Because of deforestation of the hill ranges over long periods of time soil erosion is one of the most serious problem. On account of this soil erosion not only the crop yields have gone down in the hill areas, but the areas in the plains have also been adversely affected due to situation of dams, floods, etc.

Industry

The industrial population is considerably low in this region. The so-called industries in these districts are either demand-based or based on the raw materials obtained from forests, agriculture, etc. and the produce is limited to local consumption only.

Forest-based Industries

The widespread existence of the forests has influenced the economy of Kumaun considerably. The whole region is endowed with a large area of forests. These forests provide employment to a large number of people. The main forest product-activities of this area are related to the industries like terpentine, resin, *katha*, furniture, packing cases, mats, rope making, wooden boxes, sleepers, carpentry, etc. The number of such industries registered in the Department of Industries was 122 in Kumaun as a whole. It is 83 in Nainital, 8 in Almora and 31 in Pithoragarh districts.[19]

Agro-based Industries

Kumaun region has also some small units of industries based on agriculture, livestock and horticulture. The main agro-based industries are related with edible oil, rice and rice polishing, flour bakeries, sweets and toffees, sugarcane processing,

19. The figures registered upto March 31, 1978, in various districts of Kumaon have been collected from the Office of the Deputy Director of Industries.

fruit processing, dairy goods, etc. The total number of such registered small scale industries is reported to be 159 in Kumaun as a whole. In the case of Nainital district alone, the corresponding figure is 138. In Almora and Pithoragarh districts, the number of such units is only 18 and 3 respectively.[20]

Other Industries

This group includes soap making, copper and iron vessels, earthen pots, woollen goods like carpet, sweaters, cloth, shoe-making, etc. The total number of registered units of such industries as on March 31, 1978 was 100 in entire Kumaun. District Nainital has 82 units, Almora 17 units and Pithoragarh has only 1 unit.[21]

Problems of Industrial Sector

General poverty of the people of the area is one of the main hindrances in industrial development of these hill districts. Lack of investment is due to insufficiency of market. The insufficiency of market is due to lower purchasing power of the inhabitants and lower aspiration levels. Thus, lower income level is mainly responsible for lower investment. A new product cannot find market because market structure is poor. The figures relating to industrial units given above show that their number is comparatively very large in Nainital district because of the fact that quite a larger part of this district includes Bhabar and Tarai areas where the above mentioned problems are greatly minimized.

The role of financial institution has also been quite negligible. In this industrial field, it would be necessary to secure a dispersal of industrial growth by setting up a variety of industrial units in various places. These could be fulfilled largely in the measure in which efforts are made to strengthen the base of financial institutions. In the absence of a special survey of financial requirements of large scale, small scale and village industries, it would be difficult to say, on the basis of an overall socio-economic survey such as this whether finance constitutes the bottleneck in the industrial development of Kumaun. The main institutions providing agricultural credit to farmers in the Kumaun region are Central Co-operative Bank, Land Mortgage Bank and Primary Agricultural Credit Societies at the village level. With their expanding network of branches, commercial banks are well prepared to play a vital role in the agricultural development. Besides the financial difficulty, there is the problem of marketing. The cost of transport of the produce is substantially high. The result is that the produce cannot compete with lower products of the areas in the plains. Besides these problems, the people lack the spirit of enterpreneurship, being orthodox and traditional. The region, being

20. Ibid.
21. The figures registered upto March 31, 1978, in various districts of Kumaun have been collected from the office of the Deputy Director of Industries.

at the extreme core of backwardness, the people also lack in technical know-how of designing industrial projects.

Trends and Prospects of Industrial Sector

The scope of industrial development in rural areas depends upon several factors, viz. availability of raw material, technical knowledge, facilities of transportation, capital market and active government assistance.[22] The hill division of Kumaun with its forests, fauna and flora, its geology, particularly vast mineral deposits, climate and over all the scenic splendour, offers potentialities of industrial development.

Regional Development Board, Hill Area Development Agency and Hill Finance Corporation have been vested with the authority as well as responsibility of industrial development of Kumaun. Industries department, with its divisional and district offices, is functioning even at the block level. There is much to be done for the uplift of the economy of Kumaun. These typically backward areas need special and prompt attention in this direction. Only then, the over-dependency in agriculture which is the main means of livelihood but that too quite insufficient, may be minimized and thus, the economy may grow faster.

Social Welfare

Economically backward areas are very often also poorly endowed in respect of basic social welfare activities such as educational institutions and medical and health services. The degree of development of an area and social facilities available in it are closely related. Backward areas with poor facilities, suffer from an additional handicap, "The need for providing social amenities in backward areas has been recognized in the constitution and operational guidelines for providing these facilities have been laid down in the Fifth Five Year Plan in the form of Minimum Needs Programme."[23] Adequate attention is being paid to improve the social infrastructural facilities in the Kumaun Division. The social infrastructure includes education, medical and health facilities, etc.

Education

Education needs top priority in I.R.D. programme, because it is only through the development of the individual by means of education that a sound foundation for the I.R.D. can be laid. At present there are 2576 Junior Basic Schools, 388 Senior Basic Schools and 280 Higher Secondary schools in Kumaun Division as a whole.

22. N.C.A.E.R. *Rehabilitation and Development of Basti District*. Asia Publishing House, Delhi, 1959, p. 38.
23. Lalit, K. Sen; Abdul, L. Thalia. : *Regional Planning for a Hill Area*, N.I.C.D., Hyderabad, Swarajya Printing Institute, Secunderabad, 1976, p. 159.

Details showing the number of educational institutions and enrolment figures for 1979 may be seen from the table below:

TABLE - 21

EDUCATION FACILITIES IN KUMAUN DIVISION 1979[24]

Standards	Classes	Age Group	No. of Schools/Colleges Nainital	Almora	Pithoragarh	Student enrolled
1. Junior Basic Schools	I-V	6-10	865	1023	688	288322
2. Senior Basic Schools	VI-VIII	10-15	150	125	113	90201
3. Hr. Secondary Schools	IX-XII	11-17	90	111	70	75807
4. Degree Colleges			5	5	3	N.A.
5. Technical Education Institutes			2	3	3	N.A.
6. Teachers Trg. Institutions			2	4	2	N.A.

A comparison of the above table shows that while the situation in respect of primary education facilities is not unsatisfactory, there is nevertheless, scope for improvement. In the sphere of higher education too, the Kumaun Division is not unsatisfactory. The following table shows the literacy among the rural and urban people during the year 1979 in each of the three districts of Kumaun Division:

TABLE - 22

LITERACY PERCENTAGE IN KUMAUN IN 1979[25]

District	Literacy Percentage	
	Rural	Urban
Almora	26	68
Nainital	27.4	47.8
Pithoragarh	47.1	70.0

24. Statistical Booklets, Office of the Statistics Officer, Nainital, Almora, Pithoragarh, State Planning Department, Finance and Statistics Division, 1979, U.P.
25. Statistical Booklets, Office of the Statistics Officer, Nainital, Almora, Pithoragarh, State Planning Department, Finance and Statistics Division, 1979, U.P.

In spite of the small number of educational institutions to serve the rural localities in Kumaun, there has been a marked progress in literacy among the people during the past few years.

Medical and Health Services

Schemes under Health occupy an important place in the development of community, because as the old proverb has it 'Health is Wealth'. These include the establishment of Primary Health Centres, work under the scheme of Family Planning and extension of health education. Primary Health Centre is the first composite health unit reaching the interior areas where it was long needed. The medical and health services function is performed in the Kumaun Division at six different levels. At the lowest level are the specialized units known as the Maternity and Child Health Centres (M.C.H.) and Family Planning Centres (F.P.C.). Above these are medical sub-centres. The regular medical and health service units above the sub-centre units are dispensaries, Primary Health Centres (P.H.Cs.) Urban Hospitals and District Hospitals. The distribution of Dispensaries, Primary Health Centre, Urban Hospitals and District Hospitals in the Kumaun Division will be seen from the table below:

TABLE - 23

HEALTH AND MEDICAL FACILITIES IN KUMAUN IN 1979[26]

Particulars	Almora		Pithoragarh		Nainital	
	Rural	Urban	Rural	Urban	Rural	Urban
1. Allopathic Hospitals	47	5	39	6	44	15
2. Allopathic Dispensaries	11	-	2	-	2	-
3. Ayurvedic Hospitals	23	-	45	-	-	-
4. Ayurvedic Dispensaries	12	-	-	-	29	-
5. Homeopathic Hospitals	3	-	2	-	2	-
6. Family Welfare Centres	14	-	67	-	60	-
7. Maternity and Child Health Centres	50	-	58	-	44	-
8. Primary Health Centres	14	-	-	-	6	

Medical and public health services are, however, quite inadequate taking into account the small number of medical centres in the Kumaun Division and the large hilly tracks without proper transport facilities.

26. Ibid.

A visit to several villages in the region led us to observe that village sanitation is almost unknown to many of them. The pathways and surroundings of dwelling houses in many villages were found to have been turned into toilets, which produce unbearable stink and pollute the surrounding with extreme, unhygienic conditions which are responsible for dangerous diseases.[27]

Village Panchayats in Rural Development Schemes

Independence must begin at the bottom. Thus, every village will be a republic or panchayat having full power. It follows, therefore, that every village has to be self-sustained and capable of managing its affairs even to the extent of defending itself against the whole world. It will be trained and prepared to perish in the attempt to defend itself against any onslaught from without. Thus, ultimately, it is the individual who is the unit. This does not exclude dependence on and willing help from neighbours. It will be a free and voluntary play of mutual forces.[28]

When India became independent, it was realized that the great task of national reconstruction would be achieved only through the active and enthusiastic support of the masses. The problems of appalling poverty and widespread misery that the country inherited from the past could be solved only through an organized endeavour of the people. In 1952 when the Community Development Programme was launched, the concept of people's participation became the main plank of the programme and became an important ingredient of most of the schemes. In the earlier stages of the Community Development Programme, people displayed enthusiasm and came forward in large number to contribute labour, cash and material. Very often it was found that people's efforts far exceeded government expenditure. All the workers engaged in the programme were charged with a mission to enlist more and more people's participation. A sort of healthy rivalry and competition developed not only amongst villages and panchayats but blocks, districts and even States. Definite targets were laid down and efforts were made not only to fulfil those targets but to exceed them. But the tempo of people's participation cannot be said to have remained throughout.

Our case study of the panchayats in these localities has shown that the panchayats have helped, to some extent to develop civic and political awakening among the rural masses. The need is, as H.D. Malviya observes, "Working in an atmosphere of conflicting interests in villages, the panchayats seek to prevent violence and help peaceful transition. As decentralized units they will remain a wholesome corrective in our democratic evolution. As the medium for mobilization

27. Sah, B.L. : Integrated Rural Development, *Quarterly Journal of the Local Self-Government Institute (Bombay)*, Vol. XXI, No.2, Oct. 79-Dec. 79, Issue No. 198, p. 488.
28. Gandhiji, M.K. : *Harijan*, 28th July, 1946.

of the community, they will lead the villages on the path of self-help for development. They will harmonize conflicts through persuasion and goodwill and achieve desired results".[29]

But these objects can be achieved only when the panchayats in these hill districts are properly organized and given sufficient opportunities to evolve as natural institutions for the performance of the responsibilities entrusted to them. Subsistence level economy still persists with the characteristic poverty and sub-human levels of living standard. The situation in the hills and other backward areas is marked by acute forms of human destitution. To many of these people modern living and education have no meaning. Equally lacking is any understanding of the objectives and responsibilities of panchayat membership and readiness to use panchayats for planning and executing village development programmes. The vast majority of the rural population still depends far too much on Government initiative and assistance and has not as yet developed a strong sentiment of self-reliance and initiative, whether individual or co-operative.[30] It is a grievance of the people that planning is imposed from above and thrust on them. "There is a three-pronged race between the plan and the people. The plan tries to run ahead but the people lag behind. No intelligent interest has been created in the people. The plan is not felt by the people. There is still the hangover of the unitary system of Government."[31] It means that there is need to be more and more decentralization of power and economy. The village communities have hundreds of problems to enumerate, but most of them can be solved, though not fully, by the local organizations alone. In the scattered rural communities of this hilly region, we are faced with several socio-economic problems. These problems can very well be solved by involving local institutions and by the opinion of influential leaders in rural areas in various types of social welfare activities intended mainly to improve living conditions of the weaker sections and to make their life comfortable. Antyodaya or benefit to the poorest section of the community is the sole criterion for determination of priorities. The following table shows the progress of Antyodya Programme in Kumaun in 1979.

Antyodaya programmes need to be studied more carefully and given a fair trial by all those who are concerned with and involved in the process of planned change in Kumaun Division in this matter.

29. Malviya, H.D. : *Village Panchayats in India*, All India Congress Committee, 7, Jantar Mantar Road, New Delhi, 1956, p. 842.
30. Cf. *Evaluation Report on working of C.D. and N.E.S. Blocks* April 1957, p. 20.
31. Report of the Fourth National Conference, *Panchayati Raj, Perspective and Programme*, New Delhi, AIPP, 1964, p. 84.

TABLE - 24

PROGRESS OF ANTYODAYA PROGRAMMES IN KUMAUN DIVISION IN 1979[32]

District	No. of Selected families			No. of Accepted Plans			No. of Benefited Families		
	Families	S.C. families	Total	Families	S.C. families	Total	Families	S.C. families	Total
Nainital	4536	2464	7000	1292	1241	2533	663	620	1483
Almora	8003	4613	12616	1927	2100	4027	1454	1721	3175
Pithoragarh	5868	3582	7250	530	589	1125	530	589	1125
Total	16407	10454	26866	3755	3930	7685	2853	2930	5783

In Kumaun Division where villages are generally scattered in thinly populated and isolated localities the formal functioning of the panchayat bodies does not evoke the desired interest and popular enthusiasm among the masses. The panchayat meetings are often very poorly attended by the members and most of the resolutions which are recorded, appear to be more formalities. The panchayats have shown some interest only in such developmental projects which are financed by the Planning and Development Department.[33] The major contribution through voluntary labour in completing these development works has not always been exactly what it is estimated and propagated. But if village leadership be evolved and trained on right lines, such contributions would be available to quite a large extent. More freedom needs to be given to the village communities for proposing their own schemes.

Restricting government grants for particular types of schemes only, cannot help all the village communities who may not be requiring them. So, the government grants should be paid to the panchayats from the block budgets on population basis for general developmental purposes. The panchayats should be left free to submit their own plans to the authorities at the block level for approval. They should be free to utilize the funds at their disposal for the schemes approved by the block level authorities.

Particular attention needs to be given in the hilly areas where erosion problems can assume serious proposition if control measures are not taken up in the near

32. Compiled from the data collected in the Office of the Deputy Development Commissioner, Nainital.
33. See Chapter VIII.

future. The following table shows the progress of Food for Work Programme under Soil Conservation Plan in Kumaun Division:

TABLE - 25

PROGRESS OF FOOD FOR WORK PROGRAMME UNDER THE SOIL CONSERVATION PLAN IN KUMAUN DIVISION[34]

District	Unit	1979-80		Progress Upto 31-12-1979	
		Distributed foodgrains (M. Ton)	Financial grant as a target (Rs.)	Consumed foodgrains (M. Ton)	Grants Utilised (Rs.)
Almora	Bageshwar	-	-	-	-
Almora	Ranikhet	10.00	12000.00	3.40	4080.00
Nainital	Nainital	10.00	12000.00	2.00	2400.00
Nainital	Garampani	5.50	6600.00	0.445	534.00
Pithoragarh	Pithoragarh	10.00	12000.00	-	-
Total		35.50	426000.00	5.845	7014.00

Besides, governments efforts the simple soil conservation techniques need to be popularized amongst the cultivators through Panchayats and V.L.W's in all the blocks where the problem of eroded or user land exists.

Although, most of the land found in the hill area is rocky and forested, yet waste land which is fertile, can be brought into use for agriculture by the panchayat bodies, by inviting the demonstrators from the Block Office if needed. Of course, in these hill villages there are many natural water sources, e.g. rivers, streams and lakes, but the availability of water for irrigation is not utilized. The panchayats can make big water reservoirs by contributing voluntary labour, cash money and material not only from the village people, but also from the Government. As there is heavy rainfall in these hill areas, the water can be stored in these reservoirs by means of *gools* and pipelines and used during the time of scarcity for irrigation. The vegetable growth has been restricted by several factors and the progress has been even slower in Kumaun hills. Quite big tracts of land lying in the boundaries of revenue villages are termed *benap* or unmeasured. Farmers are not permitted to utilise these tracts for agricultural purpose. But the panchayat can utilize these tracts of land with the permission of the authorities of the Revenue Department.

34. Compiled from the data collected in the Office of the Deputy Divisional Commissioner, Nainital.

They can make community orchards or can grow vegetables on them on community basis. The problem of marketing and transportation of produce can be solved to some extent by the panchayats by buying the fruits and vegetables from all the village farmers and selling them at reasonable prices in the nearby marketing centre. To rid the problem of transportation, the produce can be used by panchayats by opening small agro-based industries. These industries will require workers and so the scheme will be able to provide employment to the village people.

If these problems are solved, Kumaun may, no doubt, be a good producer of fruits and vegetables; and horticulture might be more paying than agriculture. It will also remove the seasonal unemployment due to defective cropping pattern. The panchayats can establish through their own resources small, indoor cottage industries. Each individual village panchayat can start such industries through its own resources. For example, if a panchayat is rich in forest resources, it may start a forest-based industry like making wood implements. Many villages of Kumaon region have come forward to take improved technique in all programmes of agriculture and rural development as soon as they have been convinced by facts and practice that by adopting these techniques they would add to their produce, efficiency and common welfare.

The leadership, both the official and the non-official, has also to share the blame for their failure to enthuse the people to come forward for voluntary service. The non-official members does not play their proper role and the official member finds it difficult to divest themselves, in any large measure, of responsibility for planning. Plans are prepared at the higher and the official level and handed down to lower bodies. Planning by the people at each level in relation to their area has yet to strike roots.[35] The Block Development Officer and, more particularly the Extension Officers, became more of desk workers than extension workers.[36] The non-official leaders get busy in power manipulation. Thus, neither could bring out the innate potentialities of the people for *shramdan* and mobilize them into constructive channels.

There is a great urge in the people to contribute their mite and examples are not lacking where people are ready to contribute their share, but proper conditions to ensure their participation have not yet to be created. The call for people's participation has yet to be created. Such a call, in order to succeed, needs an environment of earnest hard work with emphasis on honesty and austerity in public life at all levels. The fact is that people's participation is an essential pre-requisite for the success of any efforts for economic reconstruction of the rural communities.

35. Programme Evaluation Organisation, *6th Evaluation Report* (June 1959), p. 17.
36. See Chapter VIII below for details.

In the present context of things no other system can help to solve the problems of community development and rural self-government better than the panchayat system can. The panchayats are the key institutions in rural localities for shouldering the responsibility of community development. But their success would depend largely upon the type of leadership they may have, the guidance they receive from the official wing and last but not the least, the cooperation they get from the people who compose them. In the hill districts of Kumaon Division, when most of the village panchayats have been organized in scattered and thinly populated individual village communities with very poor economic conditions, we noticed that young generation is tending to leave the village in search of jobs elsewhere in town or in the plains. Hence, the panchayat leadership continues to be in the hands of those people of the villages who are either disinterested or frustrated, and have no faith in panchayats and their working. Official leadership in respect of remote parts of the rural localities seems to be satisfied with the routine activities. People participation in planning and executing the schemes of rural development, in the circumstances mentioned above, appears to be non-existent in most localities. This is the basic problem with which the panchayati raj and development both are faced.

One great problem is that the masses of people who dwell in the rural hill areas are living in conditions of extreme poverty and illiteracy. They are ill-organized and lack knowledge for effectively participating in programmes of their own betterment. I.R.D. focuses attention on the fact that the country as a whole will not progress, no matter how fast is the progress in the fields of industry, transportation, railway, shipping, etc. unless the rural areas progress in the same measure and with equal speed.

5

PEOPLE AND PANCHAYATS

General Level of Political Conciousness Amongst the Masses

"W.H. Morris Jones has been sceptic about the rationale and potentialities of democratic decentralisation (popularly known as Panchayati Raj) for providing substance to democracy and ensure speedier development at rural local levels. He, however, concedes that Panchayati Raj has introduced an element of competitiveness which should help in the emergence of new leadership with new styles, which in turn, should provide a new start to democratic and development process."[1] Panchayati Raj has increased the pace of political consciousness both among leaders and people in the rural areas which thus so far had been held insulated from the national main stream. The horizontal and vertical mobility of leaders under Panchayati Raj and growing exposure of the people to the outer world to fulfil their developmental needs have been a contributing factor in this process. The role of Panchayati Raj leaders, as opinion leaders, has further buttressed their influence. Panchayati Raj has also offered an opportunity to the rural people to choose their own rulers at the local level. This, in turn, should be helpful in internalizing the value of vote on the one hand and evaluating the performance of their own rural local leaders in comparison to the State level and national ruling elite, on the other.

The process has, however, been handicapped due to tardy growth of institutionalized patterns of role, behaviour and sense of political responsibility commensurate with political consciousness. The Panchayati Raj organization consisting of village panchayats, the Samitis and the Zila Parishads mean extension of leadership resources at the disposal of the people. Panchayati Raj institutions can initiate an overall planning, mobilization of people and resources, and to look after the general administration at the local level.

Since 1947, when India got political independence, the percentage share of rural elite in national level power politics-position has increased. Samuel P. Huntington who otherwise has been over-sensitive to the issue of political order and stability, has made a significant observation in this regard, when he says, "In modernising countries the city is not only the focus of instability, it is also the

1. I. Narain and Others : "Democratic Decentralisation, Some Political Consequences", *The Economic Weekly*, Special Number, July 1962.

centre of opposition to the government. If a government is to enjoy a modicum of stability, it requires substantial rural backing. The support for the ruling party comes from the countryside, the support for the opposition comes from the cities."[2] These observations appear quite correct in so far as the conditions in India are concerned. The present regional study of Kumaun hills concerns itself with the political behaviour of panchayat leadership in terms of their participation in elections, the extent and bases of their influence and the perspective guiding their behaviour in planning and executing the I.R.D. programme. In this context the role of political parties has also become quite significant.

An interesting dimension reflecting upon the role of psychic factors in politics relates to considerations motivating persons in joining a party. In the course of our present study, a query to this effect was administered to panchayat leaders of some development blocks in Kumaun hills, whose replies on this score are represented in the following table:

TABLE - 26

MOTIVES FOR JOINING A PARTY[3]

Parties	No. of respon-dents	Freedom move-ment	Principles of party	Village develop-ment	Political and per-sonal con-sideration	None in particular	Total
Congress	100	5	7	22	38	28	100
Janata	100	-	-	35	24	41	100

As the table is self-explanatory, no detailed analysis is called for, except for the comment that personal and political considerations play a greater role in making a person join a party than do the ideological considerations. The replies in the category of 'none-in-particular also indicate the same trend. The pattern of responses preference for Janata Party is "Congress was degenerated. It was corrupt. So, I joined the Janata Party". Or "I was interested in politics. The party provided the avenue to do so". Moreover the "Janata-wave" motivated persons in joining the Janata Party.

Majority of people were not found to be happy with political leadership. The table below indicates their unhappiness with the MLA who, as ex-officio member of the Kshettra Samiti, is supposed to take an active part in all round development

2. Samuel P. Huntington. : *Political Order in Changing Societies*, New Haven : Yale University Press, 1970, p. 435.
3. Survey conducted in 21 sample village panchayats of different blocks in Kumaun.

of the area. It is very unfortunate that the bulk of people seem to think that the politicians, though aware of their problems, do not want to do anything for the villages.

TABLE - 27

THE ROLE OF POLITICAL LEADERSHIP (MLA) VIS-A-VIS PANCHAYAT LEADERSHIP[4]

Question	No. of respondents	Yes	No	No Answer	Total
Is the MLA aware of your problems ?	100	68	24	8	100
Is the MLA enthusiastic in R.D. activities ? (Rural Development)	100	20	64	16	100
Is the MLA selfish ?	100	56	32	12	100
Do village leaders belonging to different political parties know your problems ?	100	24	56	20	100
Do they take active interest in I.R.D. programmes ?	100	20	64	16	100
Are they selfish ?	100	68	16	16	100

So far as purely political activities are concerned, a common villager is not interested in politics. Only a few who have their own axe to grind or who have chosen politics as a career are interested in party politics, and have become primary members of some of the major political parties.

The respondents, therefore, were asked if they would like to abolish the Panchayati Raj, and if so, what alternative they prefer. The responses of people in the sample survey are presented in the following table:

TABLE - 28

DIFFERENT ALTERNATIVES TO PANCHAYATI RAJ[5]

No	Abolish				Total
Abolition	Administration by Govt. Servants	Village Head with appointed Staff	Village Commune	No Answers	
65%	15%	5%	10%	5%	100

4. Survey conducted in 21 sample village panchayats of different blocks in Kumaun.
5. Survey conducted in 63 sample village panchayats in 7 sample blocks of Kumaun Division.

From the above table, it would be evident that the majority want to retain Panchayati Raj because they have a different concept of economic development which is quite different from the political activity. They feel that economic prosperity cannot be attained merely through administrative activity but through forums of democracy.

On ascertaining the popular opinion about the Panchayati Raj institutions as forums of democracy, it was noticed that the people by and large, have faith in them. The following table presents the position:

TABLE - 29

PEOPLES' OPINION ON PANCHAYATI RAJ AS FORUM OF DEMOCRACY[6]

	Question	% Yes	% No	% No Answer
1.	Participation in Panchayat elections	78.55	21.45	-
2.	Are elections necessary ?	70.00	5.55	14.45
3.	Is the present P.R. better than traditional Panch Parmeshwar ?	60.66	20.33	19.00
4.	Are the P.R. Institutions useful for rural development ?	80.33	10.00	9.66
5.	Is the Sabhapati impartial ?	60.00	20.00	20.00
6.	Will you re-elect him ?	50.33	35.66	14.00
7.	At the time of election do you consult anybody ?	40.66	49.33	10.00

From the above table, it is clear that majority of respondents (70 per cent) feel that Panchayat elections are necessary and 78.55 per cent are participating in the elections. An attempt was made to find out the factors influencing their voting behaviour and it was found that 40.60 percent respondents consult others and take various factors into consideration while voting. It is a remarkable fact that 49.33 per cent exercise their vote freely. The following table indicates that 42 per cent of the respondents, while consulting give first preference to their kins and the village leaders and friends occupy second or third choice.

6. Survey conducted in 63 sample village panchayats in 7 sample blocks of Kumaun Division.

TABLE - 30

PREFERENCE FOR SEEKING ADVICE[7]

Particulars	Ist preference (3)	2nd preference (2)	3rd preference (1)	Total Score	Rank
1. By your kins	16	-	-	48	1
2. On persuasion by Village leader	5	-	-	15	2
3. On persuasion by friends	3	1	1	12	3
4. Of your Family Members	2	-	-	6	4.5
5. On the initiative of the Caste Leader	-	3	-	6	4.5
6. On being asked by Politicians	1	-	-	3	6

The analysis of socio-cultural and political factors like age, caste, occupation, income, education, etc. in relation to leadership in P.R. institutions, implies that some of these factors are important for leadership.[8]

Table 31 shows the factors which determine the choice of the people at the time of voting. Respondents give first preference to age and experience and second to the personal qualities and education of the candidate. A study of score distribution indicates that there is big gap between first and second choice, and political ideology has no significant influence. From the present analysis, a conclusion can also be drawn that in rural areas of these hill districts economic status of the candidates has little importance.

7. Survey conducted in 63 sample village panchayats in 7 sample blocks of Kumaun Division.
8. S.C. Jain succinctly writes, "A study of the characteristics of Panchayat leadership is important for three reasons. Firstly, the performance of the panchayat as a human group depends much upon the experience, outlook and attitudes of the members upon which it must draw while it makes decisions. Secondly, leadership development is a very important responsibility of Community Development Agency. The achievements in this respect can be verified by reference to the changing characterisitcs of panchayat leadership. Thirdly, the functioning of the panchayat as a democratic organization of the community depends upon the nature of to-and-fro relationship between the voters and the office-bearers of panchayats, the characteristics do indicate the dynamics of power in a community, change of power may be a cause as well as a consequence of social change taking place within the community." (*Community Development and Panchayati Raj in India*, Bombay, Allied Publishers, 1967, p. 294.)

TABLE - 31

FACTORS CONSIDERED AT THE TIME OF VOTING

Particulars	Ist preference (3)	2nd preference (2)	3rd preference (1)	Total Score	Rank
Age, Experience	40	5	5	135	1
Personal Qualities	5	21	15	72	2.5
Education	5	23	11	72	2.5
Political Ideology	3	3	7	22	4
Caste	3	-	2	11	5
Economic Status	-	3	2	8	6
Personal interest	-	1	-	2	7

It is evident from the above table that there is no evidence to show that panchayat leadership is caste-oriented. Neither through electioneering nor through behaviour could we conclude that casteism in these hills had any important role to play. This is also because of the fact that these individual village panchayats are composed mostly of the people belonging to one or two castes only. This raises a question of alternative leadership. If a new generation of higher educated panchayat leadership is to come up in these villages, a better plan of training of the panchayat personnel, both official and non-official, and opening institutions of higher education may open the avenue of bringing in an alternative leadership.

Prominent media of political consciousness amongst the masses are through newspapers, radio, urban contacts, and village Chopals.[9] A study of our survey schedule from different places shows that the media maximally used are 'urban contacts' (70 per cent), followed by the radio (60 per cent), 'village chopals' (30 per cent) and 'newspaper (20 per cent). The high response for 'urban contacts' is obviously because of greater socio-economic mobility among the villagers of these localities in recent times.

What is lacking at the local rural level is, however, the growth of formal institutions providing a platform to the villagers to enable them to acquire greater confidence, have a more effective voice; and thereby a more meaningful participation in the management of local affairs than what they have today. These formal institutions can be the Gaon Sabha, local units of political parties, a farmer's club, and the like. However, as our study reveals, these institutions are mostly in poor

9. A study of 100 survey schedules from various villages of different Blocks in Kumaun undertaken by the author.

shape in rural hill areas. Even the Gaon Sabha, a key institution in the Pachayati Raj system, is hardly used as a forum of expression of popular opinion. Extension services as well as local party units need to pay attention to fill the vacuum, if democracy is to have some foundation at the grassroots level. Political consciousness among the rural masses is necessary, if not a sufficient condition for accelerated I.R.D. There is an important balance, which can act in a mutually constructive manner, to be struck between central power and support for local agencies, and local initiative and resource mobilization.

People's Participation in Panchayat Activities

Broadly speaking, the word 'people's participation' is used to refer to the role of members of the general public, as distinguished from that of appointed officials, including civil servants, in influencing the activities of government or in providing directly for community needs. It may occur at any level—from the village to the country as a whole.

Everyone accepts the wisdom and the need of people's participation and their involvement in planning and executing the schemes of rural development at the grassroots level. The necessity and desirability of such active participation by the people is not only the question but also the idea and its implementation which need more attention than they have so far received. It is well known that the public is not a harmonious entity; in reality, it comprises groups with conflicting interest. "It seems necessary to reiterate that the people can make a contribution to the planning process only if they are presented with a well articulated and feasible framework of approaches, objective measures and alternative."[10]

Under the three tier structure of Panchayati Raj institutions, the village panchayat constitutes the primary unit. The general body of this primary unit generally known as Gaon Sabha constitutes the village assembly and its executive is known as the panchayat. The Sabha or the assembly has the status of a body corporate and enjoys legal sanctity. The panchayat has the duty to carry out the resolutions of the Sabha. Thus, every adult citizen of the village has a voice in the Sabha and he can express about any matter of public interest under the competence of this body. In theory, therefore, full participation of the people in the management of the local affairs of the village including development is ensured. But the main problem that confronts an observer is that of its effectiveness, which depends partly upon the method of composition of these bodies and partly upon the interest the people in general take in the working of these bodies.

10. Anand Sarup : 'Planning Machinery', *The Indian Journal of Public Administration*, Vol. XXIV, 1978, p. 930.

Our observations in respect of all hill districts of Kumaun show that the Gaon Sabha meetings are attended hardly by about 20 per cent of its total members. Women's attendance is almost nil. Thus, people's participation in the Panchayati Raj presents a very dismal picture. No doubt, a smaller executive body is supposed to work more efficiently within the framework of the panchayat, but in the case of bigger panchayats, due to large absence of the members from its general body meetings, the peoples participation as a whole, cannot be ensured through a small number of their representatives. In most cases, the attendance of the members in the meetings of the Gaon Panchayats (the executive body) also hardly remain upto 35 per cent.

General policies relating to village development plans are formulated at the higher national and State levels. The local bodies have to prepare and propose their developmental schemes in accordance with these general policies, pertaining to different types of activities, viz. agriculture, animal husbandry, rural reconstruction, education, co-operation, health, industries, etc. for their respective areas. What actually happens in these lowest levels is that the panchayat bodies are made to propose only certain special types of activities in their areas for which grants can be made available to them from the planning budgets. In the course of our field study we were told that[11] the staff, i.e. V.L.W. and the panchayat secretaries insisted upon the village panchayats to propose particular types of schemes, in which the people were not actually interested. Thus, the schemes were either not at all proposed, or the people took little interest in their execution.

There is large scale absence of the members of village panchayats in their meetings. The result is that the people also do not take much interest in arranging for themselves the civic amenities and other local self-governing activities. Some people tend to show individualistic attitude rather than communitarian feelings in devising and carrying out certain activities.[12] Our study of survey schedules confirms that people's participation in rural democracy has been conspicuously lacking. Whatever available is through pressure imposed from outside. Unless people show spontaneous interest in proposed various activities of local self-government and development, the whole programme of I.R.D. is likely to meet an utter failure.

Another aspect of the people's participation in the community development programme is their contribution through physical labour in executing minor development schemes. The panchayat institutions have to propose and execute a

11. Personal enquiries made in the three sample village panchayats (Synora and Bongidhar panchayats in Almora and Jantwal panchayat in Nainital district)
12. Cf. Tewari, G.D., op. cit., These conclusions were derived by the said author in respect of panchayats in the whole of Kumaon in 1960. Our study shows that the position instead of improving has further deteriorated.

number of village development schemes. These activities include construction of roads, wells, buildings, tanks and maintenance and repair of existing projects. In the execution of such activities, village panchayats in these hill districts have not shown any systematic planning. Some panchayats, however, organize Shramdan drives from time to time for such activities.[13] These minor schemes of rural development have appealed to the people to be of genuine benefit to them and, therefore, their contribution has shown welcome response. This shows that in order to evoke popular interest and participation in planning and executing various schemes of village development the village leadership should propose such schemes first, as may clearly indicate their genuineness and desirability for the benefit of these people. This aspect of popular participation in rural development programmes needs to be given more encouragement by village leadership and this can enthuse available rural manpower to participate in activities of self-help and development.

However, the panchayats nowadays are not taking genuine initiative in planning various schemes of rural development. The present position is that a large number of public buildings, irrigation tanks, channels, community orchards, roads, water pipelines, etc. which were constructed some years past need proper maintenance in order that they might be of some use to the communities. These projects could be maintained if proper drives of voluntary labour were organized by the panchayats. But the latter have not been taking much interest in them. The result is that the money, labour and time spent on them has proved to be sheer waste. In order to promote systematic planning for the I.R.D. in these hill villages, the communities and the panchayat institutions need proper training and encouragement.

A well organized scheme of people's participation in developmental activities needs a larger degree of cooperation between the official and the non-official elements attached to panchayat institutions. The tendency on the part of one element claiming superiority of position and status over the other will hamper and destroy the very essence of the whole schemes. In this respect, people's participation has to be understood in terms of co-operation by the people and their representative bodies with the official wing of the Panchayati Raj Organization. The latter should be very careful about not ignoring popular demands and initiative. Genuine and spontaneous people's participation is a true measure of democracy. It is only then that direct democracy can adequately function.

The plans for local development are received from above and even when the local body plays some part in determining them, the role of the non-official seems to be passive. There is no attempt at an organized assessment of local needs,

13. A study of 63 sample village panchayats of different blocks in Kumaun.

resources and the adjustment of the targets to these needs and resources. In our sample study of 63 village panchayats, we observed that development schemes were received from above. Even in the few cases in which the local bodies attempted to frame the plans, the initiative and the decision were largely taken at the Block and District levels. Plans are prepared at the higher and the official level and banded down to lower bodies. Planning by the people at each level in relation to their own area has yet to strike roots.

Popular Level of Knowledge About Panchayats Functions and Responsibilities

The village panchayats constitute key institutions in the rural community life of today. They encompass the major part of village life. Therefore, the panchayats have become a key focus and one of the main concern for the study of rural socio-political life. But unfortunately, it appears that by Panchayati Raj, most of the people mean very little beyond electing the office bearers of the panchayat bodies and they feel that the development activities are the responsibility of the elected representatives or the government officials and not their own. A clear majority of the rural masses as per our study in respect of the hill districts of Kumaun Division, are unaware of the fundamentals of Panchayati Raj institutions. They do not effectively participate in the panchayat meetings. The probable reasons for such state of affairs are lack of mass awakening, endeavour by the extension agents, inefficiency of local leadership, meagre financial resources of panchayat bodies, unattractive agenda in the panchayat meetings, seasonal migration of the people in some localities, and above all the typical geographical conditions making life very hard.

The level of knowledge of the people about the panchayats is represented by the following table.

The figures indicate that about 30 per cent of respondents have no knowledge about the composition of their panchayats and a vast majority have no satisfactory knowledge of the powers and functions of the Gaon Panchayats. The possible reasons that could be given by way of explanation about such lapses are:

a) Gaon panchayat meetings are not regularly convened by the Pradhans (presidents of village panchayats).
b) Lack of interest among the people because of Gaon sabha's meagre financial resources and its unattractive agenda.
c) General poverty and hard life of the people does not enthuse them to devote time to attend the meetings.
d) Indifference on the part of village leadership in preparing an attractive programme of action for rural development.

TABLE - 32

LEVEL OF POPULAR KNOWLEDGE ABOUT COMPOSITION AND FUNCTIONS OF GAON PANCHAYATS IN KAMAUN[14]

Question on	No. of respondent	Level of Knowledge				Total
		No knowledge	Some knowledge	Fair knowledge	Full knowledge	
Composition of Gaon Panchayat election	100	32	36	24	8	100
Powers of elected office bearers	100	40	22	18	20	100
Functions of the Gaon Panchayat	100	36	20	26	18	100

All the Pradhans say that a meeting of the Gaon Panchayat takes place every month. But when the people in general were contacted they say that there is rarely any meeting every month and the fact is that the people are correct. A majority of people have lost their faith in the efficiency of the members of Gaon Panchayats and the Pradhans. On the other hand, the Pradhans blame the people for their non-cooperating attitude in the activity of panchayat for village development. The reasons may be many and varied, but perhaps, the most important has been that many of the Pradhans and the members of the panchayat bodies do not evince a sense of responsibility and the kind of primary task needed for the realization of the goal.

It does not mean that Panchayati Raj has nothing to show on the credit side. In some village panchayats, the people have shown satisfactory knowledge about the composition and functions of Gaon Panchayat as shown on the following page.

These figures indicate that majority of respondents have satisfactory knowledge about the composition and functions of the Gaon Panchayats. "Panchayati Raj institutions have yet to fulfil their promise and to translate that faith into a living and pulsating reality so that people's power is harnessed from the Gaon Sabha to the Lok Sabha in a steady progression. The inadequacies of the Panchayati Raj movement flow from lack of confidence in the system, by scanty resources and meagre responsibilities. These institutions have also suffered a serious set-back in the absence of regular timely elections."

14. These figures are based on personal observations made in the few sample village panchayats of different blocks in Kumaun and replies received from the respondents in the course of the sample study.

TABLE - 33

LEVEL OF POPULAR KNOWLEDGE ABOUT COMPOSITION AND FUNCTIONS OF GAON PANCHAYATS[15]

Question on	No. of respon-dent	Level of Knowledge				
		No know-ledge	Some know-ledge	Fair know-ledge	Full know-ledge	Total
Composition of Gaon Panchayat election	100	19	31	27	23	100
Powers of elected office leaders	100	23	12	28	37	100
Functions of the Gaon Panchayat	100	20	27	23	30	100

By and large, our study as a whole reveals that generally the people understand very little about the actual role of the panchayats. In these circumstances, the fate of I.R.D. seems to be quite dark as people's participation is the major fundamental need in implementing the integrated rural development plan. To make panchayats more vigorous and viable politically and to make them development-oriented, the following points need stress:

a) The meetings of Gaon Panchayat must be held regularly. The present study tells about village folk's unwareness of basic information like election, powers, functions, etc. This deficiency can be made up if the A.D.Os. (panchayat) regularly visit panchayat areas and enlighten the Pradhans and the people about the fundamentals of Panchayati Raj.

b) One major problem that comes in the way of development is the problem of panchayat finance. Although the Act provides for Gaon Fund to which all receipts of the panchayat are to be credited and the money so realized is spent in the activities of the panchayats, yet the panchayats do not take genuine interest in enriching the Gaon Fund. This aspect of the problem needs more care.[16]

c) It was noticed that the Pradhans are inactive in discharge of their functions. To remedy this it may be said that:

   i) Soon after panchayat elections, the Pradhans should undergo 'training' on subjects relating to agriculture, animal husbandry, and so on and also

15. These figures are based on personal observations made in the few sample village panchayats of different blocks in Kumaun and replies received from the respondents in the course of the sample study.

16. See Chapter VII, Financial Involvement in I.R.D. Programme.

on matters relating to local self-governing activities by panchayats and on how to raise funds and evoke response of the people.

ii) The A.D.O. (panchayat) is rarely found discharging this important function and to enthuse the Pradhans to convene and conduct meetings regularly to motivate the people.

d) In these hill areas, it is difficult to establish village panchayats having larger population because the small village sites are scattered. If they are joined together to constitute a bigger village panchayat, that would create more difficulty for the people to assemble easily in meetings. Sometimes the interests of the people of one village clash with those of other contiguous villages. Hence, it is feared that such clashes in the panchayat meetings may prove detrimental to the cause of community development schemes.

The villagers can do much for improving their lot if they have leaders who can bring dynamism in their lives. In the absence of such leadership nothing substantial can be achieved.[17] Leadership is quite necessary to influence people to cooperate towards a common goal and to create situations for collective response.

From another angle, the very success of P.R. institutions depends largely on the quality of leadership available at the grassroot levels. "Political development and democratic growth depend on the local leadership and its functioning in the P.R. institutions."[18] The successful functioning of village panchayats depends upon the availability of "resourceful, imaginative and active panchayat leadership."[19] The quality of leadership will ultimately determine the success and failure of P.R. in I.R.D. programmes.

What emerge here is that leadership both at higher and local levels, is interested more in capturing and maintaining hold over power positions than in holding to any specific ideological stance. In the bargain for power they get stuck up with status quoism instead of becoming an agent of accelerated social change. Neither party cadres nor panchayati leadership is either socialized or compelled

---

17. The Subject Rural Leadership or to be more specific Leadership in Panchayati Raj Institutions has attracted attention of many scholars in India as well as abroad. Some important works are : S.R. Mehta, *Emerging Pattern of Rural Leadership*, New Delhi, Wiley Eastern Private Limited, 1972; Iqbal Narain and Others. *The Rural Elite in an Indian State*, Manohar Book Service, New Delhi, 1976; Avtar Singh, *Leadership Pattern and Village Structure; A study of Six Indian Villages*, Delhi, Sterling Publishers, 1973; B.S. Bhargava, *Grass Roots Leadership*, New Delhi, Ashish Publishing House, 1979; Harjindar Singh, *Village Leadership (A case study of Village Mohali in Punjab)*, Delhi, Sterling Publishers, 1968; *Emerging Patterns of Rural Leadership in Southern Asia* (Report on an international Round Table Conference), Government of India, N.I.C.D., Hyderabad, 1965.
18. Sirsikar, V.M.: *The Ruling Elite in a Developing Society, A study in Political Sociology*, Orient Longmans, Ltd., 1970, p. 1.
19. Inamdar, N.R. : *Functions of Village Panchayats* in Jeorge Jacob (Ed.), *Readings on Panchayati Raj*, Hyderabad, N.I.C.D., 1967, p. 43.

by the demands and pressures of objective socio-political reality to play this role.

The reasons for the failure may be many but, perhaps, the most important has been that none of the parties involved evinced a sense of responsibility and did the kind of primary work needed for the realization of the goal. In this respect, perhaps, the state level political leadership is the most to blame. They used P.R. as an instrument in the game of politics and never allowed the kind of autonomy needed for its success. In order to vitalize the panchayats, village leadership needs more impetus, encouragement and training for I.R.D. programmes.

6

ROLE OF LEADERSHIP

Character of Village Leadership

"Politics has an integrational role to play. It tends to knit individual choices around certain universal norms and keep the centrifugal forces at low ebb. Amidst the confusion wrought by pressures of multiple groups, politics manipulates and crystallizes the alternatives. This may lead to a situation of differential mobilisation, trends towards which have already been identified in India."[1] It is desirable to study this phenomenon by trying to find out how Panchayati Raj leaders mobilise the people in rural areas.

The structural strength of the nucleus institutions of Panchayati Raj—panchayat, Kshettra Samiti and Zila Parishad—lies in their ability to throw up the right type of leadership which could hopefully activate Panchayati Organizations to benefit all people, including the weaker sections of the community, under common programmes of development. This purpose can be viewed as a function of the 'institutional role' allotted to the panchayat institutions and their members. To evaluate this, it is essential to apply to two-fold test of leadership - a qualitative test and an empirical test. The first calls for an assessment of the capacity of the leaders of Panchayati Raj to fulfil the role assigned to them as members of panchayat, Kshettra Samiti and Zila Parishad, and the second, an assessment of how these leaders have actually discharged their role in practice. Thus, there are two criteria for judging the leadership pattern of panchayati raj institutions: the one quantitative and the other qualitative. The quantitative criterion can be spelled out in terms of regularity and frequency of meetings, attendance of members, duration of discussions and so on. The qualitative criterion is built around the points which form the main core of discussion and decision and the level at which they are tackled. The two are, however, interlinked in such a way that they overlap each other. The discussion which follows is devoted to an analysis of the leadership pattern of Panchayati Raj from quantitative and qualitative considerations.

---

1. Narian, I., and Others : *Rural Elite and Elections in an Indian State*. (National Publishing House, 1976, p. 3.

Quantitative Analysis

There are wide variations in the number of meetings and proportion of attendance in different panchayat meetings. The following table, showing the frequency of Gaon Panchayat meetings in 21 selected panchayats, reveals that the minimum and maximum number of panchayat meetings held in 1978-79 were 6 and 12 respectively. It also shows that there were no quorum in about one-fourth of the meetings held.

TABLE - 34

FREQUENCY OF GAON PANCHAYAT MEETINGS, 1978-79

Block	Gaon Panchayat	Panchayat Meetings called (No.)	Percentage	Postponed for want of Quorum (No.)
Bhimtal	1. Jantwal	8	47	3
	2. Ranibagh	12	67	1
	3. Bhanwali	9	42	2
Ramgarh	1. Boharkoat	12	53	2
	2. Naikana	7	47	2
	3. Uriya	9	47	2
Haldwani	1. Loharyasoal	12	63	2
	2. Ramnadunga	11	57	3
	3. Bithoria	12	51	4
Bhikiasen	1. Synora	10	50	2
	2. Hawali	6	53	1
	3. Burkinda	7	52	2
Salt	1. Kornidhar	12	48	-
	2. Bongidhar	10	52	1
	3. Methani	9	60	2
Pithoragarh	1. Gurna	11	46	1
	2. Naini	10	35	3
	3. Vasti	7	39	2
Berinag	1. Kotgari	10	52	4
	2. Bhuwneshwar	11	62	3
	3. Lohathat	9	49	1

All the Pradhans say that the monthly meeting of the Gaon Panchayat takes place regularly. But when the people in general were contacted they say that there is rarely any meeting and the fact is that the people are correct. A majority of people have lost their faith in the efficiency of the Pradhans. On the other hand, the Pradhans blame the people for their non-cooperating attitude.

The agenda of panchayat meeting is neither pre-planned or circulated to the members nor affixed on the panchayat notice board. As a result, the so-called Gaon Panchayat meetings have no genuine programme for discussion in most of the panchayats. Thus, the formal monthly meetings do not attract the village leaders towards panchayat activities. The paradox is, that though it is very difficult to hold a Gaon Panchayat meeting, once a meeting begins it is seldom a dull event, as all matters ranging from local gossip to government administration are discussed. Though the panchayat is mainly in-charge of development work and civic amenities, all types of problems encountered in the panchayat area are discussed in these meetings. The average village considers panchayat to be an all purpose service institution.

Kshettra Samiti

The U.P. Kshettra Samitis and Zila Parishads Adhiniyam empowers every Kshettra samiti to hold meetings at least once in every two months. In the case of the Kshettra Samitis studied, the provision was mainly used to cover such issues as discussion of budget. The following table shows the number of general and special meetings held in 1978 and 1979 by the three Kshettra Samitis studied.

TABLE - 35

FREQUENCY OF KSHETTRA SAMITI MEETINGS

Kshettra Samiti	General Meeting	Special Meeting	Total	General Meeting	Special Meeting	Total
		1978			1979	
Bhimtal	6	2	8	5	2	7
Salt	3	3	6	4	1	5
Berinag	4	1	5	4	1	5

Not a single meeting had to be adjourned for want of quorum. The attendance was generally high. It seldom fell below 50 per cent. The Pramukhs were always present. While the meetings of Kshettra Samiti are well attended, they are not held in time. Usually the proceedings started as soon as the requisite quorum was reached; others joined as and when they arrived. The attendance of district level officers at the Kshettra Samiti meetings was generally poor. This can be seen from the table below showing the record of the three Kshettra Samitis :

TABLE - 36

ATTENDANCE RECORD

Departmental Representation	No. of meetings attended (Kshettra Samiti)		
	Berinag[2]	Bhimtal[3]	Salt[4]
District Development Officer	-	-	-
Agriculture	-	3	-
Animal Husbandry	1	2	1
Cooperation	1	2	1
Irrigation	-	1	-
Medical and Health	2	-	-
Social Welfare	1	2	1
Education	1	-	1
Small Savings	-	1	-
Assistant Collector	-	-	-
Ayurved	1	2	-

The table shows that most of the district level officers do not attend the meetings. The average attendance appears to be very low. In fact, in most Kshettra Samiti meetings the non-officials regretted the absence of district level officers. The attendance was more in Bhimtal Kshettra Samiti as compared to the others, but it was unsatisfactory in all cases.

The agenda usually consists of those items which the Kshettra Samiti officials wanted to bring to the notice of its members. Some idea of the frequency and nature of agenda items can be had from the following features relating to Hawalbagh Kshettra Samiti under study:

The meetings of Kshettra Samiti are, by and large, held in a peaceful and orderly manner. The Pramukh acts as the Chairman of such meetings. Active participation of members in the Kshettra Samiti meetings is rather limited. Only about half-a-dozen members usually take active part in its deliberations. This is

2. Total Number of meetings held in 1979 - 7
3. Total Number of meetings held in 1979 - 5
4. Total Number of meetings held in 1979 - 5

TABLE - 37

THE FREQUENCY AND ITEMS OF AGENDA - 1979

Item	Frequency[5]
Finance and Budget	7
Agriculture	6
Cooperation	4
Construction Works	3
Panchayat	2
Adult Education	1
Administration	2
Supervision	2
Recoveries	1
Animal Husbandry	2
Primary Health Centre	1
By-Laws	-
Others	10

mainly due to the fact that most members rely on their leaders to plead on their behalf. In all the Kshettra Samiti meetings, there was not a single instance of a member being denied the right to speak whenever he or she wanted to speak, though the number of speakers remained small in all the three cases. On many occasions, the Pramukh and the B.D.O. requested all the members of express their views, and no efforts were made to stop or postpone a discussion if the members felt inclined to discuss in detail. It was, however, noted that the Pramukh and the B.D.O. took more than half of the discussion hours. The co-opted members, especially the representatives of Scheduled Castes participate very rarely in these discussions.

Zila Parishad

The Zila Parishad is required to meet for the transaction of business at least once in every two months.[6] The development plan of the district in the first instance is prepared by the Karya Samiti and Mukhya Adhikari lays such plan before the Niyojan Samiti. The Niyojan Samiti may make such recommendations in the matter, as it thinks fit, and then submit the same to the Adhyaksh for being laid before the Parishad.[7]

5. Total No. of meetings held was 9. The figures have been compiled from the agenda of these meetings.
6. Section 61.
7. Section 63.

The attendance of members in the Zila Parishad meetings is high. It exceeded 60 per cent of the total membership. The President was present on all occasions. The M.L.As seemed to take greater interest in attending the meetings of Zila Parishad than in Kshettra Samitis. As far as the M.P.'s are concerned, their attendance is rather low. All the district level officers of various departments who are the members of the Zila Parishad do not care to remain present in all the meetings. Some of them often depute their subordinate officers to attend the meetings. The departments which often failed to send their representatives were the Forest, and Co-operation.

In a number of cases the representative members complained about their indifference. The Zila Parishad even passed formal resolutions in two or three cases, asking the representatives of certain government departments to attend its meetings. The members also complained that the departmental representatives did not come fully prepared to deal with the cases about which the Zila Parishad required their advice or suggestions. Even then no fair response have been taken by the departments.

From the point of view of leadership behaviour, it could be safely concluded that the state of affairs is quite satisfactory at the Kshettra Samiti level, though the situation is not ideally perfect. The Kshettra Samitis are to play an important role in the three tier structure of Panchayati Raj.

Qualitative Analysis

Panchayat

A qualitative appraisal of the leadership pattern of panchayat shows that:

1. The members of the Gaon Panchayat are, by and large, indifferent to its activities. Even when they attend panchayat meetings, they normally prefer to toe the line of Pradhan and would most often not participate at all. There would hardly be an occasion when they would take any initiative in the deliberations of its meetings. They are not active partners to the decision-making process.
2. The utility of Panchayati Raj institutions is not appreciated by those below the level of Pradhan—those who may be called the panchayat incarnate. This has naturally made the Pradhan a very important and powerful functionary who is tempted to misuse his position by the sheer docility of other panchayat members.
3. As a corollary to this, the panchayats in these hill districts have failed to enthuse or activise the villagers through ward panchayat members who themselves are inactive.

The lack of interest or involvement and participation on the part of panchayat members should not, however, be taken as an argument for discrediting the Panchayati Raj mechanism. If the panchayat members are assigned some specific responsibilities, it will be a significant step in the direction of activising them. Their activisation has however, to be accepted as a slow and a long drawn process.

Kshettra Samiti

The extent of leadership in the Kshettra Samiti also does not go beyond a few Pramukhs who are more vociferous than others. Most members of Kshettra Samiti remain passive receivers of information, toeing the line of action that is suggested to them by the Pramukh or the Block Development Officer. It may be noted, however, that whenever the Pradhans of village panchayats, who are members of the Kshettra Samitis participate, they bring local orientation on their observations, spotlighting thereby the problems and difficulties of their areas. They thus serve as true representatives of their respective areas and hence fulfil one of the important objectives of Panchayati Raj, namely spotlighting the needs and problems of the local people.

Most of the Kshettra Samitis have been monopolized by the Pramukh or the Block Development Officer (depending on their personality), or by the both. Little effort has been made by them to encourage participation of other members.

Sometimes a deputy of the District Development Officer attends the meetings of Kshettra Samitis. His presence in the meetings adds to the interest and enthusiasm of the members. The impact that he creates usually emanates from his involvement and interest in community development and Panchayati Raj. It also depends on his attitude towards villagers and their problems in general as well as his capacity to communicate himself to the villagers.

It is very difficult, again, to suggest any means of improving the leadership pattern of Kshettra Samiti in terms of better participation by members or better performance by officials. This, again, has to be accepted as part of a process which will find its own way, still the following suggestions may be useful, though it is difficult to provide for them statutorily:

1. The Block Development Officer and Pramukh should try to elicit maximum participation of Samiti members.
2. The training imparted to the officials should emphasize the importance of identification with the programme and their imbibing what is commonly known as 'development orientation'. To further encourage this, 'development orientation' need to be treated as one of the grounds for their further promotion in their service career.

Zila Parishad

As far as the qualitative aspects of the behaviour of Zila Parishad members is concerned, the following observations have been made:

1. Most of the M.Ps. did not attend the meetings of Zila Parishad and those who cared to attend them seldom felt inspired to participate in the deliberations. Of course, whenever they participated, their participation was of a high order from the point of view of the content of ideas that they conveyed and the suggestions they made.
2. As far as the M.L.As are concerned, they took keener interest in the meetings of the Zila Parishad. By and large, however, their contribution was more in terms of debating skills than that of ideas and constructive suggestions.
3. The Pramukhs are most articulate, politically and functionally, of all the non-officials in the three tier structure. Thus the extent and level of their participation at the Zila Parishad level had been better than those of the Pradhan and the other members at the panchayat levels. Still actual participation and deliberations had been limited to a handful of Pramukhs. Others had remained silent spectators.
4. As far as the performance of the district level officers is concerned, it has not made any impact, because they send their deputies, who are not well briefed. Generally they were not in a position to give full information about the various issues that were posed to them by the Zila Parishad members.

To sum up the local political processes should get differentiated from higher level political processes. The local political elite should not just be on the receiving end of the dictates of the higher level elite. Otherwise, there will be no safeguard against the misuse of power by higher level authorities, as it is the role of intermediate[8] leadership to exercise restraint on them. Local leadership is also a restraining influence on the people. It not only acts as a reference group for popular behaviour, but it also channelizes the demands on the macro-system.

"The intermediate leadership provides an additional tier to the leadership structure and its strengthening would enhance the adaptability of the organizational network and thereby provide a functional safeguard against the vagaries of mass politics as its very existence may imply certain restraints both for the national elite and the people."[9] It is for this reason that a wide variety of philosophers and scholars including Gandhiji, M.N. Roy, Jayaprakash Naryana, Tocqueville, David Truman, Robert Dahl, etc. have been votaries of decentralization of powers to

8. The term 'intermediate' leadership is being used here as synonymous with local leadership in the sense that it is placed in between the people and higher level elite.
9. Narain, I. and Others : *Rural Elite and Elections in an Indian State*, op. cit., 1976, p. 3.

provide a basis for the strengthening of intermediate structure and leadership.

Of course, the village leadership is governed by the influence wielded by dominant socio-economic interest. It is expected that the Panchayati Raj would help the emergence of democratic and development oriented leadership which would imply changes both in its orientation and structure. It would be broad in outlook and would strengthen the process of change towards social justice and an egalitarian social order which are part of the democratic system as envisaged in the preamble to the Indian Constitution.

Administrative Leadership

"Administration plays a sort of second fiddle to the popular leadership in a democratic set-up. But then the administration and the political processes get intermingled; resulting in a politicisation of administration and administration of legal and constitutional sobriety to politics which may tend to go haywire otherwise. The administrator has the right to be consulted, to encourage and to warn, besides his duty to implement the constitutionally validified policy. The duty of the administrator is all the more onerous today since policies are laid down and implemented pending legislative ratification ex-post-facto."[10] The day-to-day concern of the panchayat leadership is offered by local bureaucracy, the members of which are associated with the developmental activities in the countryside. In fact, both the popular and administrative wings are equally charged with the responsibility of efficacious administration of community development programmes.

In the working of the whole programme of I.R.D., leadership occupies a place of prominence without which one cannot conceive of any fruitful results. This leadership may be classified in two heads—official and non-official. Non-official leadership is offered mainly by the people's representative bodies and the office-bearers of these bodies, and sometimes by outside elements too, e.g., the workers and leaders of political parties, other popular elements, not actually representing the panchayats, and the general public opinion. Whereas official leadership constitutes the whole body of administrative and extension service personnel belonging to different departments (administrative and developmental) posted in field stations at various levels, (village, block and the district). This official leadership has a very significant role to play in the whole Panchayati Raj set-up which has the responsibility of rural Local Self-Government and Rural Development.

The discussion which follows seeks to bring out the aspect of Panchayati Raj through a 'structural—functional analysis of its leadership, the latter being classified

10. K. Seshadari, "The unresolved Debate of Centralisation vs. Decentralisation", *The Indian Journal of Public Administration*, Vol. XXIV, No. 3, 1978, p. 677.

in four broad types—parent members, co-opted members, associate members and additional members.[11] The classification of membership so made, is based according to the method by which it is constituted at different levels of Panchayati Raj, including the rights and privileges which are statutorily guaranteed to it.

Parent Membership

The Pradhans and Up-pradhans and Panchayat members are the directly elected functionaries in Panchayati Raj. Yet, as it will be borne out from subsequent discussion, the Pradhan and Up-pradhans are the least articulate members of the Panchayati Raj set up of hill areas.

The parent members of a Kshettra Samiti are those who are Pradhans of its constituent panchayats. There is an important aspect pertaining to the duality that goes with the office of Pradhan who is both the head of panchayat and an ex-officio-member of Kshettra Samiti. The present members of the Zila Parishad are the Pramukhs of the constituent Kshettra Samitis.

To sum up the findings of the foregoing analysis, it may be said that Panchayati Raj has been instrumental in throwing up a new type of local rural leadership. The leadership is drawn mainly from the ranks of agriculturists and money lending classes. The Panchayati Raj institutions have failed to activise the large bulk of female population who perhaps have very little chances of securing electoral success on account of the compulsions of social backwardness in Kumaun region.[12] There was not a single parent woman member in the sample Kshettra Samitis which we studied. In fact, no women tried to contest for a seat.

As far as the influence of caste is concerned, it appears that there is no evidence to show that panchayat leadership in these hill districts is caste-oriented. Neither through electioneering nor through behaviour can we conclude that casteism had any important role to play. This is also because of the fact that the hill villages are composed mostly of the people belonging to one or two castes

11. Included in these categories are : (1) Parent members. At the panchayat level, Pradhan and Up-pradhan who are directly elected to the panchayat; at the Kshettra Samiti level - all Pradhans of village panchayats who are ex-officio members of Kshettra Samiti; and at the Zila Parishad level—all Pramukhs of Kshettra Samitis who are ex-officio members of Zila Parishad. (2) Co-opted members: All those who are co-opted as members in the various panchayati raj institutions and enjoying all participatory voting and office holding rights. (3) Associate members: The Members of Parliament and State Legislatures enjoying associate membership (without voting or office holding rights) of Kshettra Samitis and Zila Parishads covered by their constituencies. (Quoted from Mathur, M.V., and others : The emerging Institutional leadership, *Panchayati Raj in Rajasthan*. Impex India, New Delhi, 1966, p. 25-26).
12. By the study of 100 sample questionnaire.

only. Moreover, the caste loyalties are cut through by the formation of power alignments and interest groups based on factors other than caste. This should ultimately strengthen the democratic base in Kumaun.

Co-opted Membership

Co-optation is done by the present members after nominations are invited. In this context, it may be emphasized that a candidate for cooperation has to be proposed and seconded by a member of Kshettra Samiti, that is, by a Pradhan. Consequently, only those persons who can enlist the support of at least two Pradhans can expect to get themselves co-opted.

In none of the three Kshettra Samitis women were coopted. In fact, no such women were available. As far as co-optation of representatives of scheduled castes is concerned, the need to co-opt such persons did not arise in a large number of Kshettra Samitis. Either such persons had already become parent members of panchayats or the population criterion for co-optation of scheduled caste were not fulfilled. Thus, co-optation at the Kshettra Samiti level with regard to scheduled caste and women representatives is only a marginal device. The persons co-opted from the Managing Committees of cooperative societies fulfilled the statutory qualifications only nominally. They were in no way distinguished in the field of cooperation and failed to provide any expert advice in this matter to the Kshettra Samiti. Thus, co-operation of members of the Managing Committees of co-operative societies also does not make any material difference to the working of Kshettra Samitis or of the cooperatives.

The election of Pramukh takes place after all co-optations are made, the candidates for pramukhship were always interested in securing co-optation of their own supporters so that their voting strength might increase. In fact, co-optation assumed great significance as the candidates for pramukhship themselves wanted to secure membership through co-optation.

Thus, as far as the specific categories of co-optation go it is clear that in these hill districts co-optation of women and representatives of scheduled castes has not served any genuine interest, except giving a formal representation to the backward sections of the society. The experience with co-optation has also been unhappy in the functional context. The co-opted members do not take any active interest in the Kshettra Samiti affairs. They have been more or less silent spectators or have toed the line of the dominating group. The persons co-opted as representatives of scheduled castes would attend the meeting fairly regularly but would rarely participate in the discussions.

The provision of co-optation of three to five women and three to ten persons each from scheduled castes has been made applicable in the case of Zila Parishad also. The experience of Zila Parishad, however, shows that such a provision is rather superfluous. Co-optation in this regard takes place if no parent member of Zila Parishad belongs to these categories. Since associate members (M.L.As and M.Ps) are also treated as parent members, there is hardly any need for co-optation of members belonging to scheduled castes.

If we are not to take a cumulative view of co-optation in relation to the three tiers of the Panchayati Raj structure, the overall picture appears to be rather depressing. The following general observations can be made in this regard.

Co-optation does not result in the addition of any specialist or expert in the real sense of the term. It also does not leave much scope for genuine representation of depressed classes or of women at any level. The motivation behind co-optation is not to secure genuine representation or real expertise but to add to group strength. It may be pointed out that as far as the representation of depressed classes and women is concerned, the fault does not lie entirely with co-optation. These sections of rural society are neither articulate, nor have they become interest groups. This makes it possible for the members of the dominating group to manipulate and co-opt them to suit their own political requirements. As these sections become conscious and politically articulate, the chances of misuse of this category of co-optation may probably decrease.

The experience with co-optation has also not been happy in the functional context. The co-opted members did not take any active interest in the Kshettra Samiti affairs; they remained more or less silent spectators or toed the line of the dominating people. The persons co-opted as representatives of scheduled castes would attend the meetings fairly regularly but would rarely participate in the discussions.

Associate Membership

All M.L.As whose constituencies cover the Kshettra Samiti area are associate members of Kshettra Samiti. The M.L.As. are almost invariably present in Kshettra Samiti meetings. The category of associate membership has been particularly meaningful in the case of Zila Parishad. Here, the total number of associate membership is very large, in fact, even larger than the total number of parent members. The associate membership at the Zila Parishad level consists of M.Ps. and M.L.As. As far as the M.L.As. are concerned, they showed more interest in the working of Zila Parishad than the M.Ps. They were also more regular in attending its meetings than the M.Ps.

If, however, one were to look at the category of associate membership strictly from the point of view of creative contribution both at the Kshettra Samiti and Zila Parishad levels, it could be said that generally the associate members have not made any substantial contribution in terms of constructive criticisms or suggestions. In spite of this, the associate members have a promotional role to play. They constitute a joint forum representing local, state and national interests.

The M.L.As may take local issue to the State Legislature and the M.Ps. to the Parliament. As the Panchayati Raj institutions get firmly rooted, the associate members will have to discharge their promotional role. The chances of their political survival will then be closely linked with their ability to forge happy relations between the Panchayati Raj structure and the state and national legislatures.

Co-optation of a representative of co-operatives at the Kshettra Samiti level is sound in principle. It embodies an attempt to forge a link between the cooperative and the Kshettra Samiti. This category of co-optation should, therefore, continue. It can be, however, mentioned that harmonious relationship between the cooperative and Kshettra Samiti has not yet developed.

The administrative leadership is responsible for the successful execution of the development programmes at the local level. The administrator has not merely to implement but also to educate. As the administrative leadership occupies a prominent place in the working of rural development activities, there would be no I.R.D. in the villages of hill area. That a need for mutual understanding between officials and non-officials exists because the officials and non-officials are both essential wheels of Panchayati Raj.

One thing which needs emphasis here and the serious attention of the policy makers and implementers is the fact that the weaker sections (which include women also) do not get sufficient representation on these institutions. Naturally, their interests are not properly represented and safeguarded. The provision of co-optation in practice does not serve the purpose, partly because co-opted members more often than not act as 'yes men', partly because of the inferior status they enjoy in the stratified rural social structure. In brief, they do not come up to expectations. The field experience suggests that their role in decision-making process in Panchayati Raj institutions is almost nil. Many a times, scheduled caste and women co-opted members do not turn up to attend even meetings (general and budget) of these institutions. It is, therefore, necessary to give second though to the provision of co-optation for the weaker sections in these institutions. There is certainly a need to evolve more effective means and methods so that the weaker sections are sufficiently represented on these institutions and their interests are properly represented and safeguarded. This will amount to a deliberate move to accelerate change in local power structure, in the desired direction.

Role of Leadership in Planning and Execution of the Schemes of Rural Development

The importance of leadership in every walk of organized life, needs no explanation. It is more important in the context of P.R. institutions because of the urgent need of proper leadership suited to development needs of the countryside. Commenting on the role of leadership, Iltiza Khan states, "Leadership is thus sine qua non of success in all human activities but in a democratic system, particularly at the lower levels, it assumes greater significance and wider proportions."[13] It is natural, therefore, to expect from these institutions that they would throw leaders who could act as catalytic agents for I.R.D.

The functional achievements of Panchayati Raj leadership and institutions can best be studied by grouping them into two separate but inter-dependent wings. Officials and non-officials. The non-officials are the elected or co-opted representatives of the people. Their role in Panchayati Raj institutions has, therefore, to be somewhat different from the role of officials who constitute a permanent cadre. The non-officials can only provide general guidance from the standpoint of the people and maintain overall supervisions over the working of Panchayati Raj institutions. The officials, on the other hand, have to work out the details and enthuse and guide the people to implement the schemes according to the decisions taken in the general meetings of the Panchayati Raj institutions.

The non-officials and officials, however, work in different spheres of 'decision-making' and 'policy implementation', though their role and activities are inter-dependent particularly because in reality both are associated more with implementation than with 'decision making'. The officials have to play a significant role in guiding the non-official element especially on technical and specialized matters with a view to help the non-officials to take right decisions in the broader context of national plans and local needs. The non-officials in Panchayati Raj institutions are men of sound common-sense and local knowledge. But their wisdom has to be supplemented by expert advice based on specialized knowledge which trained officials alone can supply. The non-officials have to act as pathfinders. The officials even with their special training cannot make much headway against age-old practices and psychological resistance of the people to modernization. Most of the schemes executed in the seven Kshettra Samitis which we studied were suggested or 'sponsored schemes' of the Government Departments. The latter also provided the funds for the implementation of these schemes. The departments, in other words, drew up the general details of a scheme and sent circulates to various Kshettra Samitis for its execution. Generally, none of the

13. Khan Iltiza : *Government in Rural India*, Bombay, Asia Publishing House, 1969, p. 96.

schemes could be executed at the block level without the association of panchayats.

Having selected the location for the execution of a departmental scheme, the Kshettra Samitis left it to the official wing to carry it out according to the instructions of higher authorities of the department concerned. The only other way in which Kshettra Samitis exercised any control over the schemes was to review their progress. Even this was done either at the initiative of the department which informed the Kshettra Samitis that a particular scheme was not making much headway or at the initiative of some Pramukhs who complained about the implementation of such schemes. The discussion which follows provides an account through an examination of the operation of each important or major scheme of development.

Agriculture

The Panchayati Raj institutions are expected to promote agricultural development in every respect. For this purpose, an agricultural extension officer (A.D.O. Agri.) is posted in each Kshettra Samiti. He is assisted by Gram Sevaks (V.L.Ws) who are expected to devote their time for agriculture.

Most of the schemes relating to agriculture are formulated by the Agricultural Department of the State Government and are passed on to Kshettra Samitis for execution with the help of panchayats. Among the schemes transferred are demonstration and distribution of various types of implements, fertilizers, manures appliances, seeds and disbursement of various types of agricultural loans and grants for specified purposes.

Seed Distribution

The Agriculture Department recommends the seeds which are to be purchased by each Kshettra Samiti and also specifies the vendor and the price. The Kshettra Samiti is only empowered to make suitable changes. The work of distribution of seeds has been handled most unsatisfactorily. In most of the Kshettra Samitis there were allegations against the V.L.W.s that the improved variety of seeds were distributed only to the people acquainted with him.

Fertilizers Distribution

Considerable emphasis has been placed on maximizing the use of fertilizers. Kshettra Samitis generally fix targets for this purpose. Despite their best efforts, consumption of fertilizers has, however, remained low. The major shortcomings which we noted in this regard are: unwillingness on the part of panchayats to bear transportation costs and lack of irrigational facilities.

Plant Protection

Plant protection schemes are sought to be popularized by demonstrations and distribution of implements. Kshettra Samiti has also to arrange for weddings, sparying, etc. As far as plant protection schemes are concerned, the Kshettra Samitis generally did very little to fulfil their obligations. Most of the schemes were in paper and the targets generally underfulfilled.

Taking an overall view of the various schemes of agricultural development, it is clear that the Panchayati Raj institution in these hill districts have not been able to come to grip with some of the administrative bottlenecks on the one hand and resistance on the part of the cultivators on the other. At present, Panchayati Raj institutions are being used mainly as distribution centres. The extension of loans and grants involves many claimants among whom only a few can be satisfied. Naturally the Pradhan and the dominating people share a large part of the benefits. The non-officials often behave in a partisan way while the officials even when they are aware of the irregularities prefer to remain silent.

The members of Kshettra Samiti are interested in securing their own benefit than providing local guidance to the people for the promotion and development of agriculture. The village level worker, for example, does not receive much cooperation from the panchayats and has to work on his own. The agricultural extension officer at times is able to command some respect and, in some, cases, can even inspire confidence and cooperation. But his role as a specialist on agricultural problems seldom comes into play. The contents of post-agricultural schemes are dictated from above.

Social Education

Social education is another sphere of activity of the Panchayati Raj in order to impart knowledge of the role and responsibilities of the people in working the system. One of the major responsibilities of the social education staff is to organize night classes for illiterate or new-literate adults. The programme, however, has failed to register any significant progress due to a number of causes, the more important of which may be listed as follows :

1. To hold night classes it was necessary to have a suitable venue and provide for some sort of illumination.
2. Most villagers could not bring themselves to accept the idea of joining adult education classes after their day's strenuous work.
3. The literacy drives were confined only to males. The idea of enrolling female adults to such classes was never tried. Also no efforts were made to organize separate literacy classes for women.

Public Works

Grants and loans for public works, for example, construction and repair of roads, gools, etc. are channelized, through the Panchayati Raj institutions. The major difficulties affecting the progress of these schemes are listed below:

1. The funds meant for public works are very often not utilized for community use but for personal benefit.
2. Despite repeated reminders, progress reports of public works completed were not submitted in time by the panchayats.
3. Technical supervision of the works under execution is difficult, as Kshettra Samitis have only one Overseer who is not able to tour the entire Kshettra Samiti area for supervising the construction progress. In many cases the Pradhans and other local people are able to complete a work, but they find that it does not meet the technical approval of the Overseer due to minor disagreement.

Besides these activities, panchayats and Kshettra Samitis are entrusted with several miscellaneous functions, ranging from collection of vital statistics to the distribution of controlled items like cement and sugar. The institutions are often regarded as part and parcel of the official administrative machinery as agents of the government. Most of the functions thus delegated are, however, taken up by the Panchayati Raj institutions.

Relationship Between Panchayats and the Development Personnel

In a country like India whose 80 per cent population lives in rural areas, the effectiveness of any rural development programme depends most upon the rural extension services who are to help and guide these local bodies in implementing the rural development programmes. The extension services are the link between the people in the countryside and the government at the higher levels. This is a burning question, in the context of more backward areas as to how far these officials could fulfil the desired needs of the people. The Home Ministry's working group on Tribal Development in its interim report for the plan period has remarked that the quality of administration, in such areas was very poor. They (officials) could not prove themselves, as the main agents of development.[14]

The district officer is supposed to be the pivot round which the whole of developmental structure in the district revolves, but unfortunately he has been unable to make this his principal concern because of his being preoccupied with

14. Editorial ; "Tribal Development", *Economic Times* (Daily), June 7, 1978.

a variety of responsibilities and the law and order situation, etc. Consequently, the task of rural development in the district remains delegated to the District Planning or Development Officer. Planning Officer, in turn, delegates some of his responsibilities to junior officers of various development departments at the district level. At the bottom, are posted the V.L.Ws. or gram sevaks, who are the real planners and guides of the village development schemes. Consequently, the gram sevak occupies the key position amongst the official wing for entire rural development programmes.

Our case survey of some selected panchayats in Kumaun Division reveals that the performance of extension officers, by and large, has not been quite remarkable in these villages. Some have neglected the extension aspect of their work and have failed to communicate themselves to the villagers. They have also been indifferent towards tours, particularly in the interior it is a more regrettable thing that the extension officers become allies to group politics. Sometimes, they play into the hands of the dominating groups. For this, they alone are not to be blamed. The B.D.Os engage them in too much of office work. They are also helpless as the paper work is so heavy that they have no alternative but to fall back upon the extension officers.

So far as the execution of I.R.D. programmes at the panchayat level are concerned, it is the Pradhan in particular and other members of the village panchayat in general who are responsible for it. A V.L.W. has little to do with the actual implementation of schemes. But the two obligations are so fused in actual life that it becomes difficult to apportion either the burden of the responsibilities or the extent of blame between a V.L.W. and a Pradhan. Our case study of some selected panchayats show that the complication worsens when a V.L.W. feels that a Pradhan has no business to tamper with the scope of his activities as he is the agent of the State Government directly recruited by its own employment agency, while the Pradhan thinks that he is the monarch so far as the panchayat level is concerned and that he should supersede the V.L.W. in every matter. This confused state of affairs has come in the way of rapid progress of panchayats, particularly in relation to the developmental activities which both the Pradhan and the V.L.W. are expected to stimulate as being their joint obligation.

To conclude, we can say that in these villages of hill region there is an absence of coordination between the functions and responsibilities of a V.L.W. and the duties and authority of a Pradhan or a panchayat. So long as the relationships between panchayat and development personnel are not coordinated, I.R.D. cannot be a success because I.R.D. envisages a multidisciplinary approach in which all disciplines and organizations work in a co-ordinated way at all levels from the higher level to the ground level.

Administrative Co-ordination at Village Level, Block Level and District level

"Co-ordination is an administrative process which seeks to bring about unity of purpose in order to achieve common objectives. Effective co-ordination, is, therefore, necessary between different units under the same organisation and between different agencies working for the common end."[15]

The purpose of co-ordination is to achieve smooth and efficient functioning, remove bottlenecks and avoid wastage due to overlapping and duplication. Co-ordination also ensures better relationship between different functionaries and institutions. Besides, some sort of checks and balances are also needed in order to achieve the objectives of coordination. "The necessity for checks and balances in any system is well recognized. An efficient and effective system of safeguards is necessary not only in the wider interest of democracy and the state but also in the interests of panchayati raj institutions themselves."[16] In devising the system of control and supervision, it should be ensured that the system of control and supervision does not unduly hamper the independent functioning and mar the initiative and discretion of these institutions. The institutions should be saved from pitfalls and dangers but should not be stopped from growing.

The introduction of Panchayati Raj necessitated a decentralized administrative framework in the districts. The district is divided into blocks, each having a Block Development Officer and a team of Extension Officers drawn from various development departments, such as Agriculture, Animal Husbandry, Cooperation, Industries, Education, Medical Engineering, etc. These officers assist the Kshettra Samiti at the block level in formulating and implementing the rural development plans. At the village level, the main responsibility of processing the development programmes is that of the V.L.W., who is a multi-purpose worker and has on an average six to ten village panchayats under his charge. The V.L.W. guides the villages panchayats in preparing village development plans and their implementation. In the framework of Panchayati Raj administration, the district level has mainly a co-ordinating and supervising role. The real initiative and powers to plan and execute the schemes lie with the panchayats and the Kshettra Samitis to be assisted and guided by the block level administration.

Co-ordination of development programme has to be organized at various levels in the village, in the development block and in the district. At each level, two problems may arise. The first is that the work of different technical departments has to be knit together so as to make a single coordinated programme. The second

15. *Report of the Study Team of Panchayati Raj,* 1964, Government of Rajasthan, para 19.1 p. 213.
16. *Report of the Study Team of Panchayati Raj,* 1964, Government of Rajasthan, para 18.1, p. 206.

problem concerns guidance, inspection, evaluation and reporting. The need for co-ordination arises on the one hand in relation to policy and allocation of resources and on the other hand in terms of the requirements of a common extension agency. The strength of a co-ordinated programme of development lies in the quality of the specialized services which are brought together. Co-ordination should, therefore, be so organized as to bring out the best in the specialist. This involves a clear appreciation of the responsibilities of technical departments at each level in the scheme of operations, and a proper recognition of their contribution to the common programme.

Acceptance of the district as a primary level of decentralization does not belittle the importance of others lower tiers. It is realized that the pattern of District Administration will remain incomplete unless village institutions are placed on a sound footing and are entrusted with a great deal of responsibility for carrying out local programmes. The development of village panchayats on the right lines has significance for several reasons. Under the impact of new developments, including growth of population, land reform, urbanization, spread of education, increase in production and improvements in communication, village society is in a state of rapid transition. In emphasizing the interest of the community as a whole and in particular the needs of those sections which are at present handicapped in various ways, village panchayats along with cooperatives, can play a considerable part in bringing about a more, just and integrated social structure in rural areas and in developing a new pattern of rural leadership.

The village and block level schemes and programmes need to be entrusted respectively to the village panchayat and the Kshettra Samiti. They ensure a balance between popular participation and popular control on one hand and administrative efficiency and financial viability on the other. The devolution should be perfect, so that overlapping and duplication of functions are avoided. Duality of control whenever it exists should be removed, and a single line of coordination and control provided for. The Zila Parishad should have full and final authority in formulating annual budgets, developmental plans, fixation of priorities and taxation. They should also be invested with all developmental functions at the district level. Similarly, the Blocks and Panchayats should also have full powers on these matters for their respective areas.

Under the existing institutional framework of Panchayati Raj and Community Development Programme the success of I.R.D. plans would naturally demand that the Block should be made the unit of coordination-cum-development. "Co-ordination pre-supposes some degree of control and it does mean certain amount of subordination of the agencies whose work is being coordinated."[17] Such

17. U.P. Evaluation Committees Report, 1959, para 2.52, p. 41.

subordination of the field services whose work has to be coordinated by the B.D.O. should confine to their being available for cooperation in the execution of the programmes of community development at the instance of the B.D.O. More administrative set-up and coordination between extension of field services at various levels would not help to solve the problems of rural democracy. The greatest need which has to be emphasized is the friendly attitude of the field services towards the local organizations, and a healthy relationship between the two, i.e. the responsibility of local bodies to make plans and policies and that of furnishing expertise and technical guidance by the extension officers.

Our study reveals that because of lack of proper incentives and promotion opportunities for the administrative personnel from the B.D.O. to the V.L.W., most of the subordinate personnel appeared to be frustrated and do not evince genuine interest in and devotion to work in these hill villages. In doing their work, these officials emphasize more the statistics and targets rather than the quality of work. The administrative unit of the Block resemble a patch-work of officials drawn from different departments. There is thus a great need to constitute a separate and integrated rural development service for those engaged in P.R. Administration which should provide for adequate incentives and promotion opportunities on the basis of merit.

If the main responsibility of development planning at the district or block or village level is left to bureaucratic hierarchy under the control of the Ministry at the State level democratic decentralization will remain an empty slogan. There is no doubt that active involvement of the P.R. Institutions in the planning process will provide a better climate for people's participation in the implementation of plan, a condition crucial to its success.

When we use the term I.R.D., we ultimately conceive of the presence of an integrated framework of administrative and development personnel to help and guide the panchayat bodies at various levels. Sometimes and more often the field services of various departments in the district, are expected to help and guide the panchayat bodies in the sphere of their departmental programmes and functions. They take instructions from the officers of their respective departments at district and higher level. But there is need to coordinate their functions. The task of supervision over different branches of activity has become larger and more complex and has resulted in increased share of time and energy of the district collector. Large scale programmes for agricultural development, expanding and improving the cooperative movement, promoting cottage industries and the development of rural community are new responsibilities of the collector. It is obvious that administrative agencies have a much larger part to play in these directions than even before.

7

FINANCIAL INVOLVEMENT IN INTEGRATED RURAL DEVELOPMENT FINANCIAL POSITION OF PANCHAYATS

Financial Position of Panchayats

"The problems of economic viability and financial administration of the Panchayati Raj institutions assume a special significance in the context of the responsibilities for promoting economic development which have been developed upon them."[1] The successful working of village panchayats as rural local self-governing bodies depends largely upon their finances. The Gaon Sabha and its executive committee, the Gaon Panchayat, are empowered to manage and control the Gaon fund. Various sources of the Gaon Fund have been provided for in the Panchayati Raj Act.[2] The Gaon Sabha can levy several taxes and fees.[3] It has also been provided that the State Government pays to the Gaon Sabha a portion of the court-fees or fines not exceeding 50 per cent of these Nyaya Panchayat.[4] The Gaon Panchayat has been given a general power to compound offences against this Act, rule or bye-law made thereunder. The consideration for such compromise must be cash which should be credited to the Gaon Funds.[5] A Gaon Panchayat can enter into a contract for collection of taxes payable to State or any local authority.[6] The other clauses of the section give the other sources of the revenue of the Gaon Sabha. Previously the Pradhans of Gaon Panchayats were empowered to retain a balance of Rs. 25.00 only and the rest of the income was credited to the Personal Ledger Account of the Gaon Sabha,[7] from which withdrawals were permitted by the district level officers only on the authority of a resolution to that effect from the panchayat concerned.[8] This lengthy and complicated process proved very inconvenient not only to the panchayats but also to the district office. Now the Gaon Funds have been totally transferred to the panchayats and the amount deposited in the local Post Office Savings Banks, and administered by the Pradhans, and this difficulty has been solved.

In Kumaun hill districts the public property belonging to the Gaon Sabha consists of some unmeasured tracts of land, which lie in the village boundary and

1. Mathur, M.V. and Others : op. cit., 1966, p. 209.
2. Section 32(a) to (k) of U.P. Panchayat Raj Act.
3. Section 37 of U.P. Panchayat Raj Act.
4. Section 39(2) of U.P. Panchayat Raj Act.
5. Section 104 of U.P. Panchayat Raj Act.
6. Section 24 of U.P. Panchayat Raj Act.
7. Section 193 of U.P. Panchayat Raj Act.
8. Rule 179 to 181 of the Rules made under the U.P. Panchayat Raj Act, as amended uptodate.

may be utilized for some common purposes by the villagers with the prior permission of the officials of Revenue Department, i.e. S.D.O. In the case of single village Gaon Sabha, the panchayat can utilize such portions of land for any of the panchayat activities easily, and no difficulty is felt in utilizing the income derived by the panchayat from such property for the development of the village. But in case of multi-village units, disputes arise in making use of such pieces of land by the Gaon Sabha as a whole because the people of one revenue village might object to the utilization of a portion of land lying in their village for such activities as may concern the Gaon Sabha as a whole.

Although the sources of panchayat income provided for in the Act are pretty numerous, yet in these hill districts the panchayats have either shown great apathy in making use of these sources of income, or the sources indicated, do not yield any income worth the name. The result is that a large number of panchayats have a nominal income. Our survey of the position in 3 Nyaya Panchayat Circles in these districts during the year 1978-79 bears testimony to this :

TABLE - 38

INCOME PATTERN OF PANCHAYATS[9]

(Rupees)

Item	Nayaya Panchayat Circle		
	Jantwal	Sanguri	Kornidhar
1. Non-recurring grants for development	80,000	75,000	93,702
2. Taxes and Fees	1,016	540	446
3. Incon e from property	-	-	1,000

The major sources of a panchayat's income is non-recurring grants. It provides a flow of minimum income to panchayats. The non-offical members of village panchayats connected with Panchayati Raj feel that the panchayats should be given a large share of land revenue or, alternatively, argue that the function of collection of land revenue should be entrusted to the panchayats so that they may be able to augment their income by collecting the commission for performing this task. Recently the U.P. Government has circulated an order from 15th June to 15th July, 1980 to impose a compulsory land revenue tax by Gaon Panchayats to increase their income.[10]

9. Data collected from the Panchayat Secretaries of respective Nyaya Panchayat Circles.
10. Panchayati Raj Uttar Pradesh No. 5/3601/80-5/225/80-Lucknow, June 6, 1980.

As far as revenues from taxes are concerned they do not show any progressive tendency. Though the State Government and the high government officers enthusiastically campaign for the imposition of taxes by the panchayats, the response of the non-officals (members of village panchayats) has not been quite encouraging. The question of imposing taxes very often comes up for discussion at panchayat meetings but the issue is generally evaded because of the intensity of existing tax burden and rise in prices.

Tax on commercial crops is another fruitful source of income but in the sample Nayaya Panchayat Circle the panchayats did not impose land revenue. These panchayats have, however, levied taxes on water, trade and irrigation. In actual practice, most of the panchayats do not receive any significant revenue on this account. Only Dadholi and Baser-Bagar panchayats in Kornidhar Nayaya Panchayat Circle under study, received income from the management of property.

Thus considering all the sources of income, the financial position of panchayats is very poor. With constant paucity of funds the panchayats rely on the Kshettra Samitis for the execution of development schemes in their area and keenly compete with one another to get as many grants from the Kshettra Samitis as possible. Though a sizeable portion of the financial resources of the local governing institutions have necessarily to come from the government, it is necessary that these institutions also raise their own resources through different methods in order to have a sense of achievement and self-reliance.

Sources of Revenue and Items of Expenditure

Financial Resources of Panchayats

"It is widely recongised that the success of the local governing units depends to a considerable extent on their financial resources and strength. No institution can prove effective and useful if it does not possess adequate financial resources to carry out its functions."[11] Under the scheme of democratic decentralization, the Gaon Panchayats, which constitute the primary unit at the village level have been vested with considerable powers to raise their revenues.[12] In addition to multifarious municipal duties like sanitation, road repairing, street lighting, etc. the panchayats

11. Panchayat Raj Finance, *Report of the Study Team on Panchayati Raj*, Panchayat and Development Department, Government of Rajasthan, para 15.1, p. 155, 1964.
12. Section 37 of the U.P. Panchayat Raj Act, 1947 lays down that a Gaon Sabha shall impose the taxes described in clauses (a) and (b) of the section and may impose other taxes and fees on rents, trade, callings, professions, animals, vehicles and buildings; sub-section (2) lays down that the taxes, etc. shall be imposed, assessed and realized in such a manner as may be prescribed by rules. The power to approve and sanction the imposition of tax or rate and to frame bye-laws vests in the Zila Parishad.

have also the responsibility of developing the socio-economic life of the people, e.g. providing the villagers with means for ensuring a higher standard of living and overall satisfaction and comfort. For the execution of these development programmes sufficient amount of money is needed, which a panchayat can raise by imposing various taxes and fees on the villagers. It has been noted that panchayats, though empowered to levy taxes, have been so slack in collecting them that large arrears tend to accumulate. The legislation on panchayats provides that such arrears could be realized as arrears of land revenues. But no panchayat dares to take such repressive steps for the realization of arrears of panchayat taxes, because it is bound to generate bitterness among the people against the panchayat personnel. Various Committees and Commissions appointed by State and Union Governments[13] from time to time to report on various aspects of taxation by the panchayats have failed to make foolproof recommendations which could be acceptable to the panchayat bodies for giving effect to them. The result is that the panchayats have developed an apathy towards imposing taxes in order to save themselves from facing bitterness. Consequently, the income of panchayats through taxes has been nominal in most cases.

The main sources of income of the panchayats in the hill division of Kumaun are as follows:

1. *Tax Revenues*

Tax on land revenue from the actual cultivators of land is imposed by Gaon Sabhas,[14] but taxes are not imposed on houses and animals. The Gaon Sabha levy tax on vehicles[15] but in hill villages there is no question of vehicles so that tax is not imposed. The number of Gaon Sabhas levying taxes on water and sanitation are very less. In fact, most of Gaon Sabhas have not taken steps to arrange for water supply or sanitation enabling them to impose such tax.

During the year 1979-80, total income of Gaon Panchayats in Nainital district from taxes of all kinds was Rs. 3,28,054 as shown on the following page.

13. a) The Report of the Study Team on Panchayati Raj Finance; New Delhi, Ministry of Community Development and Co-operation, Government of India, 1963.
    b) Report of the Local Finance Enquiry Committee; National Government, 1950.
    c) Report of the Committee on Panchayati Raj Finances; New Delhi, Govt. of India, Ministry of Community Development, 1963.
    d) The Report of the Committee on Panchayati Raj Finances, Government of Mysore, Bangalore, 1963.
14. Section 37, Kumaun and Uttarkhand Zamindari Abolition and Land Reforms Act, 1966 (In areas where the right, title and interest of intermediaries have been acquired under the Kumaun and Uttrakhand Zamindari Abolition and Land Reforms Act, 1960, a tax on actual cultivation of land not less than twenty-five paise but not exceeding fifty paise in a rupee on the amount of land revenue payable or deemed to be payable).
15. Section 37 of U.P. Panchayat Raj Act.

TABLE - 39

THE POSITION OF THE TAX FIXATION, TAX RECEIVED AND TAX LEFT TO BE RECEIVED BY GAON PANCHAYATS IN DISTRICT NAINITAL IN THE YEAR 1979-80

Rupees

Blocks	Panchayat tax fixed in year 1979-80	Concession	Panchayat tax tax collected upto 31-3-80	Balance to be realized
Okhalkanda	5818	-	5008	810
Betalghat	6623	-	6623	-
Ramgarh	7492	-	7299	193
Bhimtal	6767	6	6575	186
Haldwani	51338	-	46754	4584
Ramnagar	51682	4618	46230	1134
Kashipur	53396	-	51111	2285
Bajpur	51202	16669	32396	2137
Rudrapur	68237	-	61728	6509
Khatima	51633	-	41854	9779
Gadarpur	24983	313	22476	2194
Total	379171	21306	328054	29811

2. ***Fees***

Licence fees are generally levied from persons who carry on trade, professions or expose goods for sale in a market place or mela held in the jurisdiction of Gaon Sabhas. In rural Kumaun, the scope for practising trade and calling is not wide, and panchayats do not seem inclined to tax petty craftsmen and profession-holders.

3. ***Grants-in-Aid***

Government grants constitute a large portion of the Income of local bodies. Without such grants they would not survive. In the case of panchayats, however, no regular recurring grants are paid to them. Individual panchayats have, however, been receiving from the Development Department, Government grants to the extent of certain percentage of the esitmated cost of a project proposed by them. Under this system only such of the Gaon Panchayats have benefited as are manned by the office bearers who take interest in proposing the schemes and making approaches to the authorities of the Development Department and the Kshettra Samitis for obtaining funds. The following table shows the position of grants-in-aid paid to panchayats by the Government for Kumaon Division in the year 1979-80.

TABLE - 40

NON-RECURRING DEVELOPMENT GRANTS PAID TO VILLAGE PANCHAYATS IN KUMAUN BY THE GOVERNMENT IN 1979-80[16]

District	Plan Allotted	Utilized	Percentage	Non-Plan Allotted	Utilized	Percentage
Nainital	5,00,000	1,07,564	61.01	50,000	10,000.00	19.86
Almora	5,00,000	31,161	17.67	50,000	26,253.50	52.18
Pithoragarh	4,00,000	37,559	21.30	50,000	14,090.00	27.98
Total	14,00,000	1,76,284		1,50,000	50,342.50	

Balance not utilized upto 31-3-1980 is to be utilized later on during 1980-81.

The system of allotment of grants-in-aid from the Development budgets to all the panchayats on population basis has not been introduced. As such the panchayats have not been able to make the plans of village improvement according to their actual needs, because they are never certain about the availability of a definite amount needed for a particular scheme.

4. *Donations and Subscriptions*

Income of panchayats under this head consists of cash donations, gifts of land or buildings and subscriptions raised by panchayats from private persons for carrying out some activity. In Nainital district, such income of Gaon Sabhas during the year 1979-80 was Rs. 92012.00, which comes to 18.69 percent of their total income. The total income of Gaon Sabhas from different sources and expenditure on construction works, office contingencies, and other sources is shown below:

TABLE - 41

INCOME AND EXPENDITURE OF GAON SABHAS FROM DONATION TAX ETC. 1979-80[17]

Income (in Rupees)		Percentage	Expenditure (in Rupees)		Percentage
From Tax	328054	73.69	On Construction Works	313520	74.51
From land management Committee	23096	5.18			

16. Compiled from the data collected from the Deputy Development Commissioner, Nainital, (U.P.)
17. Compiled from the data collected from the District Planning Office, Nainital.

From Forest Panchayat	2000	0.44	On Office Contingencies	44448	10.53
From donation	92012	20.66	Others	62803	14.69
Total	445162			420771	

During 1979-80, the income of panchayats from the different sources in Nainital district was Rs. 4,97,065.00. Of this, a major share of income of Gaon Sabhas is derved from the taxes. i.e. 73.79 per cent of total income. The highest percentage of expenditure is incurred on the construction works, i.e. 74.51 percent.

The villagers of Kumaon are poor but charitable. In the villages, the constructions of Naulas, schools or other such things of common utility are undertaken by raising public subscriptions from the villagers, government grants or sometimes by indivdual effort. If the Gaon Sabhas arrange to raise some regular subscriptions and deposit the proceeds in the Gaon Fund, it would obviate the necessity of raising them on different occasions for different purposes. That would also help to develop a healthy practice.

Panchayat Expenditure

With the meagre financial resources and in the absence of any regular control on a panchayat's expenditure policy except what is embodied in the 'budget formula' previously referred to, the major proportion of the panchayat income is spent on contingencies. After meeting these expenses a majority of the panchayats have very little left for other activities. In the case of panchayats having surplus funds the major head of expenditure relates to social and cultural activities, such as operating library and reading rooms, maintenance of radio sets, seasonal contributions to local cultural associations like dramatic and singing groups and arrangements in connection with traditional festivals. Only a few panchayats are able to spend anything substantial on civic amentites, local development schemes and the like. For executing such schemes, the panchayats generally rely on the financial assistance from the Kshettra Samitis as supplemented by people's share in the form of labour or cash. The observations made here can be meaningfully interpreted with the help of table given below:

TABLE - 42

EXPENDITURE PATTERN OF PANCHAYATS[18]

Rupees

Items	Bhikiasen	Bhimtal	Berinag
1. Administration	798	910	609
2. Civic Amenities	-	487	-

18. The figures were collected from the Pradhan of the Panchayats of different Blocks in the year 1978-79.

3.	Social and Cultural Activities	307	497	187
4.	Construction	-	97	-
5.	Maintenance	201	315	-
6.	Miscellaneous	608	720	325

Thus, considering all the sources of income, the financial resources of panchayat are very weak. They are often unable to meet the minimum administrative expenses, let alone initiate any development schemes. Whatever development schemes are undertaken by the panchayats, they are largely financed by the Kshettra Samiti either out of of its own funds or community development schematic budget or grants from the State Government. The total income from all these sources is barely sufficient. It is necessary that a new financial structure of grants and loans should be evolved with a view to make certain minimum funds available on a uniform pattern to every institution and also to promote a certain measure of discretion to them in utilizing funds according to local needs.

Financial Decentralization for I.R.D.

Local Self-governing bodies have always lagged behind for want of adequate funds. Finance is the crux of the problem of local bodies. "The problem of economic viability and financial administration of the Panchayati Raj institutions assume a special significance in the context of the responsibilities for promoting economic development which have been devolved upon them."[19]

Everyone taking any interest in public affairs, whether associated with the working of local bodies or not, will come to realize that local self-government in these backward hill districts and perhaps in the whole country presents a tragic picture. With a few exceptions, the financial position of our local bodies, in general, is hopeless, as if "inefficiency" and "local body" have become synonymous terms.

It is the general view that part of the inability of the Panchayati Raj institutions to come up to the expectation lay in their weak financial resources. The Committee on P.R. Institutions appointed by the Government of India in 1978, under the Chairmanship of Ashok Mehta rightly observes that "For discharging the developmental responsibilities entrusted to Panchayati Raj institutions, the State Government should make available the commensurate funds from its total budget on a continuing basis. The non-plan expenditure pertaining to the decentralized items will be administered by the Zila Parishad. Thus, financial decentralization must correspond to the functional decentralization."[20]

19. Mathur, M.V. and Others : op. cit., p. 209, 1966.
20. *Report of the Committee on Panchayati Raj Institutions*, op. cit., Financial Resources, 1978, para IX 12.1, p. 125.

Apart from the budgetary devolution, the P.R. Institutions should also mobilise enough resources of their own. No democratic institutions can continue to maintain their operational vitality by depending upon external resources. For this purpose, all P.R. Institutions should have compulsory powers of taxation. In addition to certain compulsory taxation items, optional items should be given to the P.R. Institutions, which should be exercised depending upon the local situation. Ashok Mehta Study Team had suggested that "Apart from the taxation powers of their own, a permanent annual grant of not less than Rs. 2.50 per capita should be available to the panchayats."[21] But this suggestion does not seem to have been followed.

In view of the meagre financial resources of the panchayats, voluntary service is necessary for execution of rural development programmes. The income which the panchayats derive from taxes, fees and other sources of their own, hardly suffices for meeting the office expenses of the panchayats. The panchayats do not get regular recurring grants either out of the general revenues or a share from some particular source or revenues of the State Government. They usually get only non-recurring grants from the development budget.

The need for raising subscriptions from private persons both in cash and kind on the occasions of ceremonies, festivals and harvesting season has to be greatly emphasized. Some villages have raised the voluntary donations but the income derived from them is not paid to the Gaon Funds of the panchayat, but it is spent on feasting and worshipping of village dieties. This expenditure can be curtailed and some amenities may, instead, be provided, e.g. arranging of light on village streets, purchasing some articles of common use for the villagers, viz. utensils, petromax, mattings, musical instruments, etc. In some villages, however, such activities are being undertaken. Ranibagh and Bhawali Gaon Sabhas in Bhimtal Block, Loharyasoal Gaon Sabha in Haldwani Block and Boharakot Gaon Sabha in Ranigarh Block have done remarkable activities in this regard.

Another important aspect which must be kept in mind is the need for adequate financial support to match the requirements for I.R.D. programmes. As has been envisaged financial backing would necessarily come from the beneficiaries or the institutional sources, the structure of organizational set-up need to be such as would enable it to rise maximum resources locally as well as from the banking institutions.

---

21. Ibid, para IX, 12.6, p. 195.

Control Over Panchayat Finances

Control over panchayat finances refers to the collection, preservation and distribution of public funds, with the coordination of public expenditure and revenue.[22] In other words, it is concerned with the preparation of estimates of income and expenditure, the collection of revenue and contracting of loans, appropriation of estimated revenue income for various items of expenditure, the accounting of the income and expenditure periodically and finally the submission of accounts to the audit to ensure their accuracy as required by the Act and the Rules.

It may, however, be remarked that the efficiency of financial control depends to a great extent on the efficiency, honesty and integrity of the staff entrusted with the task of financial administration. Even the most efficient system of budgeting, accounting and auditing are bound to fail unless the people in charge of these operations are efficient and honest. Dr. Gyan Chand rightly observes, 'integrity and competence of the staff is a factor of primary importance and cannot be ensured merely by instituting the right procedure of transacting financial business and providing a system of checks and counter-checks on the conduct of financial affairs."[23]

Maintenance of Gaon Fund and its Transaction

The control of the Gaon Fund is in the hands of the Gaon Panchayat subject to the general control of the District Panchayat Officer. All money transactions to which any member of the Gaon Panchayat or Nyaya Panchayat or any officer or servant of the Gaon Panchayat in his official capacity is a party, without any reservation be brought to account. All receipts are credited in full to the Gaon Fund with the exception of authorized advances. Money due to the Gaon Panchayat is collected either by payment at the Panchayat Office or by out-door collections, or by both methods, as the District Panchayat Raj Officer may direct. Receipts for all money received are issued by the persons authorized to receive the money. Accounts of all income and expenditure of the Gaon Fund are maintained by the Pradhan. The account is closed and balanced at the end of every month and is examined and passed by the Gaon Panchayat at a meeting in the next following month.[24]

The cash balance of the Gaon Fund is kept in the State Treasury or in Savings Bank Account of the nearest Post Office.[25] The money is deposited into and

22. Gyan Chand : Local Finance in India, *Quarterly Journal of the Local Self-Government*, Vol. XXXVI, No. 2, p. 182.
23. Ibid, p. 182.
24. Rule 178 of the U.P. P.R. Act.
25. Rule 193 of the U.P. P.R. Act.

withdrawn from the personal ledger accounts.[26]

The Gaon Panchayat may sanction expenditure out of the provisions made in the Annual Estimate of Income and Expenditure upto the amount actually in hand for any legitimate purpose. No money is to be paid from the Gaon Fund, except on a requisition for withdrawal signed by the Pradhan or such other officer as may be appointed by the Gaon Panchayat in this behalf.[27]

Proper compliance of these rules depends upon the ability of the Pradhans, and the more so upon the panchayat Secretaries who actually prepare these records. But in fact, panchayats have not generally been able to follow the prescribed accounting procedure in these hill districts. Cash books are rarely posted and closed on due dates. Often, the entries and balances do not tally. Vouchers are not kept in guard files and sometimes they are not cancelled, and the payments are not attested. The receipts for the sum realised are not issued regularly though the entries are brought in the cash books. Sometimes the receipts are issued but the accounts are not accounted for in the cash books. In some cases unauthorized payments are also made.[28]

Pradhan, in their ignorance of rules and procedures about the maintenance of these account books, leave this responsibility entirely on the panchayat Secretaries. The latter are so much overworked that they do not find time to visit all the Gaon Panchayat headquarters regularly to post the account books uptodate. The inspecting staff has been very much concerned about this shortcoming of the panchayat office bearers.

These irregularities in the maintenance of the accounts are quite common and unless the Pradhans are given special training in this direction, the problem would remain unsolved. The large size of Nyaya Panchayat Circles having 11 Gaon Panchayats on the average, offers little opportunity for the panchayat secretary to cope with this responsibility efficiently.

The procedure of making payments of the government grants to the panchayats for specific activities has also contributed to the irregularities being committed by the panchayats. The panchayats are required first to complete the project to the entire satisfaction of the authority entrusted with the responsibility of issuing completion certificate. Then they have to procure the receipts of payments from the parties concerned to whom the payments are due. Thereafter, the demand for money is made to the Planning Department, supported by the vouchers, estimates,

26. Rule 179 of the U.P. P.R. Act.
27. Rule 180 and 181 of the U.P. P.R. Act.
28. These observations were made through a personal study of the Inspection Reports of some Panchayats in the sample Kshettra Samitis.

etc. This implies that the panchayats should first invest the money. But the borrowing of money from private person is subjected to objections.[29] The panchayats are ignorant of these technicalities. This problem can be solved by making advances amounting at least to one third of the sum sanctioned for a project, so that the work could be started promptly and thereafter in piecemeals in one or two instalments according to the progress of the work.

Annual Estimate of Income and Expenditure

Every Gaon Panchayat prepares an annual estimate of its income and expenditure for the year commencing from 1st April and lays it before the Kharif meeting September-October of the Gaon Sabha.[30] After the annual estimate of income and expenditure has been laid before the meeting of Gaon Sabha, the members discuss it and various items of income and expenditure are passed by the Gaon Sabha. The expenditure under every head is deemed to have been approved if passed by majority of votes of the members present and voting.[31]

If a Gaon Panchayat does not lay the annual estimate of income and expenditure before the Gaon Sabha by 30th November, or the Gaon Sabha does not pass the same by 31st December, the District Panchayat Officer is required to prepare the annual estimate of income and expenditure for that Gaon Sabha[32] and the latter is required to pass it. In case the Gaon Sabha fails to pass the annual estimate of income and expenditure so prepared by the District Panchayat Officer, it is deemed to have been passed on the 1st of February[33] next.

The prescribed procedure of preparing the budget (Annual Estimate of Income and Expenditure) is not strictly followed by majority of panchayats. In actual practice, some routine figures are noted down by the panchayat Secretaries, first in respect of Nyaya Panchayat and then in respect of different Gaon Panchayats in the circle. Thus, the budget planning by the panchayat secretaries, is merely to keep the wheel going. Their formal approval by the Gaon Sabhas has, likewise, become a mechanical affair, and in the majority of cases, the poorly attended meetings of the Gaon Sabhas do not raise any objection to these budget proposals,

29. Under Section 36 of the U.P. P.R. Act, the panchayats can borrow money from the State Government or any other Gaon Sabha only. But some of the panchayats have been taking loans from private persons for completing the projects. This irregularity has been subjected to objection by the auditors. (A study of the reports of some panchayats made by us).
30. Rule 213 of U.P. P.R. Act.
31. Rule 218-A of U.P. P.R. Act.
32. Section 42(4) of U.P. P.R. Act.
33. Rule 219(3) of U.P. P.R. Act.

because of the fact that in these proposals no such items are included as might impose any burden on the people.

These budgets are subject to the final approval by the Assistant District Panchayat Officer of the district concerned, whose assent is received as a matter of course. In fact, these Assistant Panchayat Officers cannot be expected to scrutinize the budgets of hundreds of panchayats in the district thoroughly. Hardly in less than one per cent cases did the problem of preparing the budgets for the Gaon Sabhas by the prescribed authority (Assistant District Panchayat Officers) arise.

Of course, hill villages are desperately poor, but the poverty of most of the panchayats is at least partially self-inflicted. They have been given powers to impose taxes but they do not exercise them; taxes are not collected. A multi-dimensional effort has to be made in this regard. First, its bare subsistence at the financial level should be guaranteed by the State, writing off its establishment charges.[34] Secondly, the panchayats which can raise at best meagre resources of their own should be especially assisted.[35] Thirdly, the panchayats belonging to the minority faction in the Kshettra Samitis area should be safeguarded against discrimination in the distribution of benefits by Kshettra Samitis. It should be prescribed that a minimum percentage of total funds for developmental purposes should reach every panchayat. Lastly, the panchayats should be helped to raise their own resources by taking up the responsibility of levying taxes which these institutions have been shirking for fear of becoming unpopular.

In order to provide continuity to the schemes and projects initiated by various Panchayati Raj bodies the large fluctuations in yearly receipts and expenditure should be smoothened by drawing up uniform comprehensive five-yearly plans of resources-expenditure.

To streamline the financial administration of Panchayati Raj institutions the accounting machinery should be strengthened and the system of auditing placed

---

34. The Report of the Study Team on Panchayati Raj Finances has made a useful suggestion in this regard. "A basic minimum maintenance grant of Re. 1.00 per capita should be given to every panchayat and this should be shared equally by State and Central Government." (The report of the Study Team on Panchayati Raj Finances 1963, Ministry of Community Development and Co-operation, Government of India, New Delhi, 4.24, p. 52).
35. Cf. The recommendation of the report on Panchayati Raj Finances. "Panchayats and Samitis may be classified into three or four groups according to their capacity to raise resources to ensure that proportionally greater assistance is given to poorer categories." (10.9, p. 59.)

on a more regular footing.[36] A number of steps can be suggested in this regard here. First, a system of internal audit at the intra-institutional level (that is with the help of an agency, attached to the Zila Parishad) be developed, in addition to the regular audit facilities. Secondly, the objections raised in the audit report should merit an early and serious attention of the panchayati raj institutions. The audit report and the action taken on it should be placed before the Gaon Sabha. Thirdly, the accounting procedure in regard to the panchayati raj institutions should also be simplified. The report on Panchayati Raj Finances has made a useful suggestion in this regard as follows:

"The form of panchayat accounts should be simple and should indicate independently the normal recurring receipts on one side and the committed expenditure on the other. Special grants, contributions, its own matching contribution and loans for development projects should be separately shown on the receipt side and expenditure on development works, either its own or of samiti, should be shown on the expenditure side".[37]

It is also necessary that the intimation of available funds to Panchayati Raj institutions is made well in advance so that budget formulations at the rural local levels may not be reduced to a formality, planning from below in financial terms may become a reality and there may not come about unplanned and hurried frittering away of resources on the eve of the closing of the financial year.

A true picture of the Panchayati Raj Finances would be possible only when the income and expenditure patterns of the three tiers in each district are integrated in a single map.[38]

---

36. Some of the useful recommendations of the Report on Panchayati Raj Finances in this regard are:
    i) Every panchayat should be inspected at least once in three months by Panchayat Extension Officer to ensure that there is no misappropriation or falsification of accounts (9.11, p. 57).
    ii) A weekly statement of receipts and expenditure should be sent by each panchayat to its samiti office where it should be scrutinized and filed properly (9.12, p. 57).
    iii) All receipts of a panchayat should as far as possible be deposited in a schedule or cooperative bank or post office savings bank and money for expenses drawn strictly according to rules and procedures (9.13, p. 57).
    iv) A special branch in the office of Examiner of Local Fund Audit should be organized in each State to carry out regularly the audit of the accounts of Panchayati Raj instiutions (9.15, p.58).
    v) It should be impressed upon panchayats and samitis that defects pointed out by auditors should be promptly remedied and satisfactory explanation offered to meet the audit objection (1.15, p.58).
    vi) A special meeting of panchayat/samiti should be held for consideration of the report within 30 days of its receipt and the result of discussion should be sent to supervising authority (9.15, p. 58).
37. The Report, op.cit., para 9.10, p. 57.
38. Maddick Henry : *Panchayati Raj - A Study of Rural Local Government in India*, London, Longman Group Ltd., 1970, p. 159.

8

EVALUATION OF THE ROLE OF PANCHAYATS IN IMPLEMENTING I.R.D. PLANS

A Detailed Survey of Some Selected Panchayats in Each District of Kumaun with Comments

"The Gaon panchayat is at the root of our concept of a new society. It is the root of our Constitution. The panchayat is the synthesis of all the forces of the village and must be kept free from casteism, partiality, factions and divisions, jealously and mutual quarrels. The panchayat is not the handmaiden of the Sarpanch or the Panches but is the expression of the Will of the inhabitants of the village. They have to be free from difference of caste and religion. They represent the divine power of the people."[1] The self-governing local government, there can surely be no question. It is manifest when we consider the range, the character and the impact upon the daily life of the citizen, of the functions which the local authorities carry out. On the nature and quality of the local self-government, depends ultimately the health of a national democracy.

The present study is an attempt to highlight the problems and prospects of rural development in Kumaun hills of northwestern Uttar Pradesh. Charged with the responsibility of development and uplift of the people, these local self governing units have to face certain problems in planning and implementing the schemes of development. What kind of suggestions will have to be taken in different fields of rural development is also their concern. This study tries to bring out the perceptions, altitudes, and expectations of various key actors involved in the development process as revealed through interviews made with them.

We have observed that people have lost interest in panchayat meetings, because the resolutions that were passed did not materialize. Generally speaking, meetings are rarely held because of lack of quorum. The village plan-items were generally of common nature such as drinking water, repairs of village roads, opening of primary schools, sanitation, etc. The income source are very limited and in very few cases are derived through royalties for resins from panchayat forest. It shows that there is no enthusiasm in executing the resolutions amongst the rural people because of the lack of cooperation, illiteracy and poor income sources.

---

1. Speech by U.N. Dhebar : "Inauguration of the Panchayat Bhawan", Jotwar Rajasthan, Jaipur, 13 Nov. 1955.

Table - 43 given on the next page shows the extent of popular enthusiasm Gaon Sabha meetings amongst the rural people:

The people were enthusiastic if they attended the Gaon Sabha meetings in large numbers. The table shows that more than 50 per cent of the respondents feel that people are 'not much enthusiastic' or 'not at all enthusiastic' about Gaon Sabha meetings. While 20 per cent of the respondents found people sufficiently enthusiastic, only 10 per cent reported that people are highly enthusiastic.

Unless people actively participate in carrying out the development activities, no real purpose can be achieved. Dynamics of rural reconstruction and the growth of our democratic institutions will draw enduring strength and sustenance largely from the purposeful participation of the people through habits and institutions of self-government at the grassroots. It was the hope and faith of the nation, when Panchayati Raj movement was launched some three decades back, that genuine authority, resources and responsibilities vested in those self-governing institutions will make them bulworks of democracy and nurseries of public leadership and civic concern. However, as our field observations show, the members of the rural elite group are indifferent to their developmental roles. If they could be involved in the planning process to a greater extent, they would take to the developmental role more earnestly than they are doing today. Active and enthusiastic participation of the people in activities related to the overall development of rural areas is the basic principle. Whatever programme of action is initiated, its origin needs patient listening of the people's problems and a study of the prevailing conditions and needs.

When the village people were inquired about the expected role of an ideal panchayat their responses were as follows:

TABLE - 44

EXPECTED ROLE OF AN IDEAL PANCHAYAT[2]

Nature of role expectation	150 respondents (rural elite)			
	I Preference		II Preference	
	No.	%	No.	%
1. Administration of justice honestly in petty disputes.	94	62.67	56	37.33
2. Providing civic amenities	78	52.00	72	48.00
3. Striving for development of village	87	58.00	63	42.00
4. Striving for social harmony and justice	76	50.66	74	49.33

2. Survey conducted in 67 sample village panchayats of different blocks in Kumaun.

TABLE - 43

EXTENT OF POPULAR ENTHUSIASM ABOUT GAON SABHA MEETINGS

Block	Gaon Sabha	Highly enthusiastic		Sufficiently enthusiastic		Not much enthusiastic		Not at all enthusiastic		No replies		Total	
		No.	%	No.	%	No.	%	No.	%	No.	%	No.	%
Bhikiasen	1. Hawali	3	10.00	5	16.66	17	56.66	2	6.66	3	10.00	30	100
	2. Barkinda	2	6.66	6	20.00	19	63.33	2	6.66	1	3.33	30	100
Salt	1. Bongidhar	3	10.00	6	20.00	16	53.33	3	10.00	2	6.66	30	100
	2. Kornidhar	2	6.66	6	20.00	17	56.66	2	6.66	3	10.00	30	100
Haldwani	1. Loharyasoal	3	10.00	7	23.33	17	56.66	1	3.33	2	6.66	30	100
	2. Bithoria	3	10.00	6	20.00	19	63.33	2	6.66	-	0.00	30	100
Bhimtal	1. Jantwal	4	13.33	4	13.33	18	60.00	2	6.66	2	6.66	30	100
	2. Ranibagh	6	20.00	7	23.33	13	43.33	1	3.33	3	10.00	30	100
Ramgarh	1. Bohrakot	5	16.66	8	26.66	13	43.33	2	6.66	2	6.66	30	100
	2. Naikana	3	10.00	6	20.00	15	50.00	2	6.66	4	13.33	30	100
Pithoragarh	1. Gurna	3	10.00	5	16.66	12	60.00	4	13.33	6	20.00	30	100
	2. Vasti	2	6.66	6	20.00	10	33.33	6	20.00	6	20.00	30	100
Berinag	1. Kotgari	2	6.66	4	13.33	13	43.33	4	13.33	7	23.33	30	100
	2. Lohathal	4	13.33	8	26.66	15	50.00	3	10.00	-	-	30	100

The table is itself explanatory. Majority of the respondents (62.67 per cent of responses) show their preference in favour of the traditional role of imparting justice in petty disputes of the people. Village development goes to the second priority. The rest favoured civic amenities and social justice. A study of the above table further reveals that the people give preference to administration of justice, because the traditional role of the panchayats was to give justice in petty disputes. But the actual role of the panchayats should be the all round development of rural area, rather than to provide only justice to the people in their petty disputes.

When the respondents were asked about the performance of their own panchayats their assessments were, as presented in the Table No. 45 on the next page.

The table shows that a majority (i.e. 53 per cent) of respondents (rural elite) consider the performance of their own panchayat to be 'average'. 16 per cent consider it to be ideal performance and 20 per cent say that the performance has been 'poor'. As many as 10 per cent appear uncertain about their assessment.

People's Participation in I.R.D.

"People's participation in the Community Development programmes, as generally accepted, is the contribution of the people either in cash or in kind towards the completion of the project for the benefit of the community, such as construction of approach roads, community centres, schools, seed stores, drinking water wells, pavement of lanes and so on."[3] In broader sense, this term includes participation of the people in the various development programmes such as agriculture, animal husbandry, cooperation, public health, education, social education, cottage industries, etc. To determine what exactly has been the extent and nature of public cooperation and participation in the Community Development Programme is discussed in the present study.

The concept of development of rural areas has somehow identified itself with the development of agriculture. Agriculture is the main occupation of the rural people in Kumaun hills. But fragmented land holdings, lack of irrigation facilities, traditional methods of cultivation are some of the major drawbacks of agriculture in these hills. Only 8 per cent of total cultivated area is irrigable and that too, not adequately. About agricultural development and functions of the Kshettra Samiti, one of the Pradhans of village panchayats remarked that the high yielding variety failed and local varieties succeeded in the village. The V.L.W. cannot do anything, because without irrigation facility nothing can be done.[4] Such of the Pradhans as

3. *Report of the Committee for Evaluation and on Public Participation* (U.P. 1959), Information Department, U.P., para 5.5, pp. 77-78.
4. Personal study of Village Panchayat Kunheel (Kshettra Samiti Salt).

TABLE - 45

ASSESSMENT BY ELITE RESPONDENTS OF PERFORMANCE OF ONE'S OWN PANCHAYAT

Blocks	Panchayats	Ideal		Average		Poor		Cannot		Total	
		No.	%	No.	%	No.	%	No.	%	No.	%
Bhikiasen	1. Hawali	4	13.33	15	50.00	6	20.00	5	16.66	30	100
	2. Barkinda	4	13.33	16	53.33	5	16.66	5	16.66	30	100
Salt	1. Bongidhar	5	16.66	16	53.33	6	20.00	3	10.00	30	100
	2. Kornidhar	4	13.33	15	50.00	7	23.33	4	13.33	30	100
Haldwani	1. Loharyasoal	5	16.66	15	50.00	8	26.66	2	6.66	30	100
	2. Bithoria	4	13.33	16	53.33	7	23.33	3	10.00	30	100
Bhimtal	1. Jantwal	6	20.00	16	53.33	3	10.00	5	16.66	30	100
	2. Ranibagh	15	50.00	8	26.66	2	6.66	5	16.66	30	100
Ramgarh	1. Boharakot	7	23.33	18	60.66	2	6.66	3	10.00	30	100
	2. Naikana	4	13.33	16	53.33	2	6.66	8	26.66	30	100
Pithoragarh	1. Gurna	4	13.33	14	46.66	3	10.00	9	30.00	30	100
	2. Vasti	5	16.66	15	50.00	7	23.33	3	10.00	30	100
Berinag	1. Kotgari	3	10.00	12	40.00	8	26.66	7	23.33	30	100
	2. Lohathal	6	20.00	17	56.66	5	16.66	2	6.66	30	100

are influential persons, get their plans approved easily through Kshettra Samitis. Some Pradhans do not attend all the meetings of Kshettra Samiti, because the Kshettra Samiti Headquarters are too far from their villages. It cannot, however, be said that Kshettra Samiti is useless because if it fails at one place, it succeeds at other places. The following tables illustrate the position:

TABLE - 46

WORK DONE BY VILLAGE PANCHAYATS OF BHIMTAL BLOCK IN 1980[5]

Projects			Investment (in Rs.)
1. *Hauz* Construction	8 (Nos.)	Grants by Block	18,160
2. Cleanliness of *gools*	13 (km)		
3. Construction *gools*	350.0 (mts.)	Voluntary labour	4,700
4. Fruit Plantation	4677 (Nos.)		
5. Plantation (Others)	6144 (Nos.)		
6. Construction of unmetalled road	(20.5)	Under Food for Work Programme	
7. Construction of Kharanja	12.0		

TABLE - 47

WORK DONE BY VILLAGE PANCHAYATS OF RAMGARH BLOCK IN 1980[6]

Projects			Investment (in Rs.)
1. Cleanliness of gools	64 km	Voluntary labour	4500.00
2. Plantation	16543 (Nos.)	Voluntary labour	1850.00
3. *Hauz* maintenance	6 (Nos.)		
4. *Gool* construction	15 (Nos.)		
5. Construction of unmetalled roads	4 (km)	Voluntary labour	9750.00
6. Maintenance of fair weather roads	59.60 km		

Generally, the cultivators do not pay due attention to the cleanliness and maintenance of *gools* and *hauzes*. In the absence any satisfactory arrangement, cultivators do not take any responsibility in these matters. It would be better if other Gaon panchayats are encouraged to take inspiration from the panchayats mentioned above and to take up such activities regularly in their areas. The

5. Figures compiled from the Data collected from the District Planning Office, Nainital (U.P.)
6. Figures compiled from the Data collected from the District Planning Office, Nainital (U.P.)

successful cultivation of fruits and vegetables needs the supply of good quality seed and seedling to these villagers. The development of nursery for the supply of vegetable seeds and fruit seedlings, therefore, deserve maximum attention.

The above mentioned tables show that these village people have taken interest in the community work like construction of *hauz, gools,* fair-weather roads and in cleanliness of *gools.* But despite all this, people have not yet developed the habit of maintaining these projects properly. In order that the impact of these physical improvements may be lasting, there is need not only for proper planning and execution of various works, but also for educating the people in their proper maintenance in future. While Gaon panchayats could bear the financial burden, the people should help them by subscribing voluntary labour.

Referring to various problems of the village, one of the Pradhans stated[7] that they get royalty for resin product in panchayat forest, but the Gaon Sabha can get the royalty only when some development project is proposed in the village by the Gaon Sabha. They resolved to construct a road in the village. The construction had started six months ago. Zila Parishad had sanctioned the royalty payment to the Gaon Sabha. They had also written to B.D.O. for the payment of royalty. But the B.D.O. said that their overseer would measure the work done and then only the payment would be made. The Overseer, in turn, could not be available for the job in spite of repeated requests by the panchayat. Hence the payment was unduly delayed causing much inconvenience to the panchayat. Thus, red tapism and apathy on the part of official machinery at the block level hampered the progress.

For drinking water supply in the village, the source of which lay in government forest, the same Pradhan commented, "I had to approach the D.F.O. at Almora and then the Conservator of Forests, Nainital. The Kshettra Samiti Pramukh also wrote to them but nothing has been done so far. So, the Jal Nigam which is responsible for doing these things is also helpless because until the forest department gives permission to utilize the water, the village community cannot proceed with the work."[8] About the cooperation from the V.L.W. who holds the key position in implementing the I.R.D. plans the same Pradhan observed that V.L.W. never comes to them. Pesticides are not made available.

In the course of interviews with farmers, some peculiar observations had to be made. A farmer was unwilling to use the fertilizers for several reasons. Most of them have had a bad experience with chemical fertilizers. In the past, they had used the fertilizers but since there were no rains, their crops were dried up and the fertilizers had an unfavourable effect. Some of them do feel that these fertilizers are good but they need sufficient irrigation facilities or heavy rains. Since the

7. The view has been expressed by the Pradhan of a Village Panchayat in Kshettra Samiti, Berinag.
8. The view has been expressed by the Pradhan of a Village Panchayat in Kshettra Samiti, Berinag.

irrigation facilities are negligible in these hill areas, the farmers hesitate in using the chemical fertilizers. Several of them felt that they had no money to purchase the fertilizers and seeds.

The V.L.W. who is the pivot of extension service at village level, has so far not been able to demonstrate the usefulness of fertilizers in dryland farming. When villagers were asked whether the V.L.W. would be of any help to them when he visits them, and what a V.L.W. generally did when he came to the farmer, the latter replied: "Yes, he visits us and says— 'khad dalo, beej dalo, ye karo, wo karo (use fertilizer, use seeds do this and that, etc.),' merely as a propaganda, but the does not realize the real problems and solutions therefore."[9]

Some of the V.L.Ws. who were interviewed by us felt that farmers took keen interest regarding adopting of new practices. However, a V.L.W. telling about his actual activities said that 'though they were supposed to be multi-purpose, they have now become single-purpose hands. The distribution of fertilizers was supposed to be the only raison d'etre of a V.L.W. Though they try to distribute it by hook or crook, yet even then the target was not achieved. Their annual character roll entry was made on the basis of targets achieved in fertilizer distribution. Targets were imposed on them. They were not consulted for fixation of targets even by the block authorities. They said that they have left all other activities except to try to push the fertilizers.[10]

When an another V.L.W. was interviewed, he pointedly remarked that if the B.D.O. learnt that the V.L.W. does not care to achieve the targets fixed by higher authorities for fertilizer distribution, the latter is likely to face several consequences. He will be reprimanded in the meeting of the Kshettra Samiti or Block staff meetings. No one wants to be insulted at staff meetings by achieving low targets. Sometimes varieties which do not suit the climate of a particular place and soil, are also imposed on them. He gave an example for the late paddy variety (I.R. 24). As it is a late variety, the crop stands by the time the local varieties are harvested and, therefore, it becomes difficult to save these from cattle which are left free for grazing. He also stated that 'there are no awards for merit; but only punishment for slackness.'[11]

Thus the achievement of targets seemed to be the main concern of V.L.Ws. If they go to an area where people talk of 'diggies (small reservoir for drinking water) for water, but do not talk of agricultural development, then the V.L.W. gets demotivated and appears as saying "hell with these amenities programmes". If this is the attitude of the V.L.Ws. no amount of I.R.D. can be enhanced further

9. Based upon an interview with a farmer of Bongidhar village, Salt Block in Almora District.
10. Based upon an interview with the V.L.W. of Gurna Panchayat in Pithoragarh Block.
11. Based upon an interview with a V.L.W. of Hawali village Panchayat in Bhikiasen Block of Almora District.

because I.R.D. means development of a suitable blend of three categories, viz. output-oriented activities, a proper infra-structure, welfare and basic amenities. A proper infra-structure is essential before the output-oriented activities can yield best results. Welfare and basic amenities are essential for social and cultural uplift of the people, promoting and sustaining their interest in developmental activities. This fairly highlights the basic problems that the V.L.W. confronts and his attitude towards development.

The District Agriculture Officer, Nainital, when asked about this target-setting for V.L.Ws. for distribution of fertilizers said, "If they are distributing fertilizers it means they are doing every other thing, i.e. they are educating farmers for its use, telling them about crop rotation patterns, etc. If they are unable to sell the fertilizers, it means they have failed to educate the farmers about the extension work. Therefore, distribution of fertilizer is the best criterion for assessing the efficiency of a V.L.W."

The Block Development Officer of Bhimtal, who has to his credit an experience of 25 years in the agriculture department including 14 years as a B.D.O. when asked about the problems of the area and scope of development, told us that "the development of horticulture is the primary concern in his block, for which so far no extensive programmes have been launched. Higher education of people is the next. Besides, irrigation, industries, communication and link roads, and drinking water are some essential requirements of the people."

About the concept of development and objective of planning his observations were: "Raising the standard of living, removal of poverty and want, ensuring happiness of the people are the basic objects of all development planning." As to how he thought this could be achieved in the area under his jurisdiction, he emphasized the importance of social education and noted that, "unless people were trained within a proper environment and adopt new technology, nothing could be done. Untimely supply of construction materials like cement and lack of transport facilities in villages, hamper the work undertaken by the block in villages."[12]

When asked about the attitude of people towards forestry and soil conservation, an officer of the forest department in Almora district had the opinion that, "they had tried to develop farm forestry in the area which would have resulted in better fodder and cattlefeed, would have retained moisture and given them fuel for their use; but they did not succeed because they did not have favourable response from the farmers. Only one or two persons who were educated, led the people and because of some vested interests, the development of the whole area was held up."

12. The observations of B.D.O. of Bhimtal Block.

In the hill districts of Kumaun various alternatives for development of forestry exist. One of them is to make forest panchayat and allot the area under civil forests to forest panchayat, so that the village people may also not have to face any problem, if they need the trees for their own use. Panchayats can take initiative from the Forest Department to be guided in the management of forest panchayats in their villages.

"Employment is the most important objective of industrial development in the district" —remarked the Deputy Director of Industries, Pithoragarh, when he started telling about the present condition of industrial development. He felt that there was increased awareness among the people. Referring to people's participation in programmes for industrial development, he said, "We get B.D.O. and Pramukh involved for granting loan to entrepreneurs and for knowing their (entrepreneur's) capabilities." Since industries department provides technical and advisory assistance (to some extent financial assistance also) to entrepreneurs, major financial assistance has to be arranged through banks. The coordination, therefore, between industries department, financial institutions, P.W.D., Hydel Department, Jal Nigam and Revenue Department (for land acquisition) becomes essential. When he was reminded of the fact that three major products of the hill area are timber, resin and fruits which are processed at Bareilly and consequently the Kumaun hills do not get the adequate benefit of its produce, he said, "Funds that are likely to be available to us are not known in the beginning. Our planning, therefore, is temporary. If in one particular area the unit is to be set up then for infra-structure one has to look to Hydel Department for power, P.W.D. for road development, etc. There should be different authorities but there should be one coordinator be it the District Magistrate or Planning and Development Officer. But this is lacking. Every department is going on its own way. Forest Department has got a policy of auctioning the timber to highest bidders. Bigger industrial units (like Star Paper Mills, Saharanpur) take the lead. Local bidders do not get them. When they ask for raw materials from Forest Department they refused but they are supplying to Star Paper Mills." He was of the opinion that the State Government should give the funds in advance for better planning of industrial development. He also expressed the view that because in the hill districts no big unit has been set-up, the potential for application of modern management concept has not been created. Thus, the utilization of forest resources has, however, not fulfilled the aspirations of the local population because the produce has always been sanctioned to highest bidders. Local people could not take advantage of these. This also affects the forest-based industrialization in the area.

The breed of milch cattle in rural hill area is very unsatisfactory. People could be encouraged to reduce the number of cattle with them and have a lesser number of cattle of better breed. This would again mean education of the farmer on economy of such propositions, otherwise he would continue his own traditional way. Good quality of cattlefeed will also be required. Pasture development and utilization of panchayati lands would serve two purposes-availability of fodder by growing grass and the conservation of soil.

In the hills, a network of irrigational schemes are physically and economically not feasible because of unsuitable topography and inaccessibility of water resources. It would involve a lot of expenditure in construction but the revenue expected therefrom would be meagre.

About the political interferences in implementation of rural development plans, it is said that the engineers working for some schemes are threatened by political leaders because the leaders know that no scheme could ever be implemented, no matter whoever interfered. Sometimes the officials engaged in various nontechnical development department did not understand the technical problems of projects and this leads to a difference of opinion between technocrats and non-technocrats. This makes the implementation of schemes difficult.

When the B.D.O. was asked as to whether he visited villages regularly to known the difficulties of villagers, he said: "We are supposed to have a minimum 20 days tour per month. I do visit villages regularly."[13] Later interviews with farmers in villages of the same block revealed that they did not know who the B.D.O. was. They said that Pradhan knew the B.D.O. because of the Kshettra Samiti meetings and the B.D.O. had not visited them since the time he had been posted in the block. The villages were situated in a remote valley, which did not have motorable road and involved an up and down hill journey of at least four kilometres on foot from the nearest motorable road.

One Block Development Officer was of the opinion that the work of planning must be taken away from Kshettra Samiti members because they are illiterate or ignorant. In any case, the plans have ultimately and finally to be made by B.D.O. so why give the members the power to plan? The B.D.O. supplies the technical guidance about the projects to be undertaken by the block. The B.D.O. said that he was not getting full cooperation from Kshettra Samiti members. "Pradhans are only interested in drinking water, etc. and not in agriculture or horticulture. They just do not listen to us." As against all this, the Block Pramukh of the same block was of the opinion that officers in charge of various schemes did not listen to them.[14]

It will be wrong to place the blame in exclusive terms either on the leaders, or on the people or on the official machinery. The securing of people's participation is a cumulative process and as such its reasons are several and lie much deeper.

13. These observations were made by personal enquiries from the people and the B.D.O. (Block Salt) in the field station.
14. The observations were made by personal enquiries from the B.D.O.

The Block Development Officer and, more particularly the Extension Officers, became more of desk workers than the extension workers. The non-official leaders got busy in power manipulation. Thus, neither could bring out the innate potentialities of the people for Shramdan and mobilize them into constructive channels. The village people are still willing and prepared to contribute their bit with regard to those schemes which fit in their pattern of priorities and square with their felt needs but there is a problem of mobilization and needs effort on the part of leadership, both at the official and non-official levels.

Popular Participation and Development

"Popular participation is an institutional device to imbibe a sense of sense of oneness among the people of the area in various developmental projects. It is a process by which surplus time and energy of the rural people could be constructively used in community work. If the functions of the Panchayati Raj bodies are to increase progressively, *pari passu,* public interest in its working must increase to create a base for popular participation. It has also an economic justification as capital itself is short. The post-Independence institutional design of local government system is based on this assumption."[15] But with all this, popular participation has lost its novelty and vogue in villages of Kumaun Hills. Above the level of the village panchayat, there is little enthusiasm and interest. Even at the panchayat level the extent of popular initiative is not encouraging.[16]

As far as people's contribution in the form of money, material and manpower is concerned, it is noticed that the people from the higher income groups, traders and middle class people, contributed in cash and material. In the case of manual labour or Shramdan, the higher income group naturally has supervisory duties. For the villagers from the low income groups and for the landless labourers the choice is practically restricted to manpower.

There is a distinction between 'community work' done through people's participation and C.D. sustained only through a change in the attitude of the people of the area.[17] In the absence of people's participation, community work simply becomes a show-piece or a high-pressure drive with little regard and less room for people's cooperation.[18]

15. Nandedkar, V.G. : op. cit., p. 59.
16. Cf. C.O.P.P., Vol. I, p. 5. *The Reserve Bank of India Bulletin,* Vol. 15, No. 1, January, 1961, had also expressed similar views in the Summary Review of the Community Development Programme in India.
17. Nandedkar, V. G. : op. cit., p. 163.
18. *The Seventh Evaluation Report,* New Delhi, The Programme Evaluation Organization, Planning Commission, 1960, p.121, "When the visit of the dignitary is over, the compost pits often remain unused, soakage pits are never kept in condition, and the hygenic significance of the repairs to the wells is little appreciated and it turns into a show-piece."

Public participation is public education. Without it even a well-intentioned plan becomes a mere mechanical fixture. Delegating responsibility to the elected or nominated representatives is inadequate. When people do not take interest in the affairs of the community. Shramdan becomes mere compliance with the wishes of their leaders and the government, and the sacrifices do not remain voluntary. In some villages from the sample Kshettra Samitis (Salt Block), people's rating for various social needs was as: (i) approach road, (ii) village school, and (iii) soil conservation activities. Even in scarcity conditions they showed little enthusiasm for soil conservation activities, but they were available in adequate number for road works. Some enthusiasm was, however, shown in the construction of class rooms in the village primary school.

Gaon Sabha is an institutional approach to popular participation. It provides a base for three tier structure of the P.R. Institutions. It is regarded as the grassroot organization of democracy. To J.P. Narayan, the Sarvodaya thinker, Gaon Sabha signifies village democracy. To him representative government from the village to Delhi was no good substitute for direct democracy.[19]

Whatever may be the ideal theory of Gaon Sabha, in practice, it has exposed certain limitations in its extension, certain weaknesses in its working and has developed certain unhealthy practices. The Gaon Sabha, as it stands today is, therefore, away from its Panchayati Raj context and far away from the Rousseauian ideal which J.P. Narayan has advocated.

In the course of our field study, the respondents were asked whether the Gaon Sabhas are effective or not. The responses varied and according to their frequency, they can be listed as: (1) There was a general apathy amongst the people in the working of the Gaon Sabha. (2) Villagers were divided into factions and the ruling faction monopolized the Gaon Sabha. (3) Gaon Sabha could only pass resolutions but has no machinery to secure the execution of its resolutions. (4) The elected panchayat members do not reflect the real leadership of the village.

These reflections focus our attention on the maladies of this institution. The Gaon Sabha does not function as it should have functioned. The meetings are thinly attended, quorum was seldom achieved and many times the Gaon Sabha reports were paper compliances. This was the candid confession of many of the respondents. Village factions created divisions in the Gaon Sabha and its decisions lost community support. Accordingly, Gaon Sabha decisions showed little effect on the decisions arrived at by the village panchayat. Village panchayat at times is not identical with the real and effective leadership of the village. For example, some politically influential elements in rural localities not only tend to destroy the

19. *Seminar on Fundamental Problems of Panchayati Raj*, New Delhi, All India Panchayat Parishad, 1964, p. 64.

smooth working of the rural economy, but have also put their greedy hands into the social welfare of the poor rural people. This case of individual benefit through political pressure was reported to us while surveying the village of Bajune Haldu in Haldwani block of Nainital district.[20] A bridge which had no benefit for the community was built forcibly by some influential individuals out of the grant of Rs. 8,000 realized from the cane department through pressure. Even in works undertaken by development departments the approach was to the individual rather than the village community as a whole, so that thirty years of development activity was able to influence only a fraction of the rural population. The village panchayat must take upon itself the responsibility for creating and maintaining sufficient work opportunities, in other words, for development of resources and employment. It means that the land and all the resources of the village are to be managed and developed in the interest of the entire village community. That is to say, the village as a whole is an economic unit in which agriculture and other occupation are organised by or on behalf of the community.

The Gaon Sabha thus does not live upto its expectations. Though a statutory institution, it has no binding authority. Control of the Gaon Sabha over the Gaon Panchayat is ineffective and, therefore, its educative aspect has become insignificant. "The idea of Gram Sabha, by and large, has not struck roots in the minds of the people. It has so far reached the prominent persons in the village.... The positive outlook of the prominent persons in the village on the Gaon Sabha has to be tapped and activised to bring the common people in large numbers within the fold of the Gaon Sabha."[21]

The Gaon Sabha has failed. But it is the basic institution of democracy at the village level. Therefore, it must be made successful. Democracy has been defined as 'a government in which everybody has a say'. Hence a democratic administration by a panchayat cannot be a good substitute for rural democracy until every villager effectively participates in the working of the Gaon Sabha.

20. B.L. Sah, : *Integrated Development at the Village Level, Uttarakhand Bharti (H)*, Research Journal of Kumaun University, Vol. 3, 1978, No. 3-4, p. 120.

21. Inamdar, N.R. : *Functioning of Village Panchayats*, Bombay, Popular Prakashan, 1970, pp. 76-77.

9

CONCLUSION AND SUGGESTIONS

9

CONCLUSION AND SUGGESTIONS

The overall impression of the nature, impact and prospects of the role of village panchayats in I.R.D programmes is necessary to preface the presentation of the cumulative view implied in the query with the observation that perhaps cannot avoid here repetition and overlapping of some of the views expressed in previous chapters. However, summarizing the more important findings of those chapters in a systematic way so that a synthetic overall portrait of the role of village panchayats in I.R.D. may be drawn.

Panchayati Raj: Genesis of the Concept

Prelude

The concept of Panchayati Raj has developed from the idea of a close knit village community to that of an organic base for a three fold revolution—social, political and economic.[1]

Panchayati Raj was inaugurated in Uttar Pradesh on 15th August, 1949 with faith and hope which were widely shared by people. The concept of P.R. found an important place in the Directive Principles of State Policy in the Constitution of India. The trend of slowing down in popular enthusiasm for Community Development Programme necessitated fresh thinking and fresh approach. The recommendations of the C.O.P.P were aimed at ensuring economy and efficiency in the C.D. Programme and enabling democratic bodies to take over the entire general administration and development of the district or sub-division. It was in this overall context that the Central Government appointed in December 1977 the Committee on Panchayati Raj Institutions under the chairmanship of Asoka Mehta to suggest measures to strengthen the Panchayati Raj Institutions. This report, was an important landmark in the history of Panchayati Raj in this country. Unfortunately till today, no effective action has been taken on this report.

On 19th May, 1979 in the Conference of the then Chief Ministers, it was decided that a Committee of the Chief Ministers might prepare a draft for a model of Panchayati Raj Act under the chairmanship of the Agriculture Minister of Government of India.

1. Nandedkar,, V.G. : *Local Government Its Role in Development Administration*, Delhi, Concept Publishing Company, 1977, p. 1.

The conference of Chief Ministers agreed on the following points:

1. The present three tier system may be continued.
2. Elections of the Panchayati Raj bodies should be held regularly. If, however, it becomes necessary to supersede a Panchayati Raj body, its elections should be conducted within 3 to 6 months.
3. The tenure of the Panchayati Raj bodies must be five years.
4. The Panchayati Raj bodies may be given sufficient powers and sufficient financial resources be placed at their command.

It is a matter of regret that till now no progress has been made to draft this proposed model Act. The Asoka Mehta Committee's principal thesis is the functional necessity for decentralization of adminstration. Where millions of people are involved through a very large number of micro-projects, decentralized administration is an unavoidable necessity.

Kumaun Division is still very much backward as compared to other districts of the State, because of its situation, topographical condition, poor communication and irrigation facilities, lack of education, etc. In order to inject new ideas in them, concentrated and improved media of information and publicity has to be pressed into action. The rural communities scattered in the remote corners of the Kumaun hills can evolve themselves as free citizens of a free state by no other system than by the Panchayati Raj.

The Three Tier Structure

Of the three tier structure of Panchayati Raj, the bottom tier, the village panchayat, is obviously the foundation. The strength and vitality of the whole structure and its democratic nature would depend upon the strength and vitality and democratic nature of the village panchayat. In spite of this, each tier in its own jurisdiction is equally important as the other. The Kshettra Samiti is not more important than the village panchayat and the former not less important than the Zila Parishad. It is, therefore, not a question of deciding whether more or less power should be given to this or that tier. Each should have all the powers that it needs in order to do all that it is competent to do in its own sphere. If control of resources remains in the hands of the State Government, the devolution is bound to be rather nominal. Land revenue, even though it does not amount to very much, should be the first resource to be placed totally at the disposal of the village panchayat and the Kshettra Samiti. The success of I.R.D. in these underdeveloped and backward hill districts would depend largely upon the interest the State Government takes in giving sufficient financial assistance to different types of rural, local bodies and panchayats.

In the hill districts of Kumaun Division, where the villages are generally scattered in thinly populated and isolated localities, the organizational pattern of panchayat institutions seems to have been imposed upon the village communities from above. The composition of the panchayats has no roots in the traditional union of the village communities. There is need for undertaking a reorganization of revenue villages through fresh demarcation of village boundaries so as to make them more compact and self-sufficient in area and population. However, the reorganization of revenue villages in the region is under consideration. This would help in the convenient composition of the panchayat bodies for individual villages or groups thereof according to the needs of different tier bodies. "The unit of local government must be sufficiently small so that people can understand it. It must be sufficiently near so that people can live up to its expectations."[2]

Panchayats being the base of the pyramid of P.R., their performance has a vital bearing on the functioning of higher tiers of the system. The panchayats in Kumaun hills have not come to the expectations of the people. They have been entrusted with numerous responsibilities, but do not have adequate wherewithal to discharge them. The factors responsible for the weak position of the panchayats in these hills, include lack of proper use of resources, lack of adequate and timely guidance and supervision from higher levels, complexity of rules and procedures, group factions, etc.

Gaon Sabha is envisaged as a popular base for P.R. set-up. An active Gaon Sabha will provide a modicum of direct democracy at village level. Gaon Sabhas in this hill area have not been active so far due to variety of reasons. The formal functioning of the panchayat bodies does not evoke the desired interest and popular enthusiasm among the masses.

The popular contribution through voluntary labour in completing the development projects has not always been exactly what it is estimated. But if village leadership be evolved and trained on right lines, such contributions would be available to a large extent. There is need for giving more freedom to the village communities in proposing their own schemes, and government grants for such projects as are essentially needed by a village people, should be sanctioned liberally. More attention needs to be paid to the desirability of the maintenance of the completed projects by the concerned panchayats themselves. Restricting the sanction of the government grants for particular types of projects only, cannot help all the village communities who may not be requiring them. Hence government grants from block budgets should be paid to the panchayats generally, on population basis and the panchayats should be required to submit their own plans to the authorities at the block level for approval before they are allowed to utilize the amount of the grants sanctioned.

---

2. Nandedkar, V.G. : op.cit. p. 4.

Rural Development Programmes

Geographical, climatic and structural variation in the valleys and hill slopes of the Division have marked distinction in the social and economic condition of people. The uphill areas are full of dense forests but they have not contributed in the economic development of local people as no forest industries have been established in the hill region. The timber and forest produce are transported to industrial sites which are located outside the region. Thus, the hill economy is seen suffering from dearth of development in industrial sector and is marked for absence of manufacturing industries. Even the agro-based industries are not well developed, which can be probably because of prohibitive cost of transport, lack of inputs, skill and dearth of entrepreneurial talent.

Agriculture has not proved to be a gainful occupation in the Kumaun Division because the holdings are small and fragmented and it appears uneconomic to adopt modern scientific means of cultivation in these small and fragmented holdings. The strategy is, therefore, to diversitfy the agricultural land for the development of horticulture, which is far more profitable in the long run. The other occupation which can improve the economic condition of small and marginal farmers of the hill area is animal husbandry. Kumaun Division is predominantly a hill area which is responsible for the production of vital products like milk, meat, eggs, wool, etc. and which also provides means of subsidiary occupation to a large number of people. Though some progress has been made in the livestock development in the past, but its impact is not very significant so far. It is necessary that the growth rate in the production of livestock products should be faster than the growth rate in the human population so that per capita availability of milk, meat, eggs, etc. may increase proportionately. There is no doubt that the development of horticulture and animal husbandry will increase the per capita income of the people of the region.

The breed of good cattle need to be encouraged to enrich the farmers economy, these cattles would require better fodder, which can be utilized by village panchayats by growing grass on waste land. This will serve two purposes; first, by selling the grass village panchayats will increase their income and second, the conservation of soil will also be done.

As the result of so many constrainsts agriculture in tropical conditions as Kumaun hills at least inhibits dynmaism and drives people to fatalism, unless it is entightened from time to time by technological improvements, development of agronomical practices and suitable diversification. Linking agriculture with industry (cottage or small scale industry including processing industry) is also necessary for the same end, so that there should be change from a purely agricultural society to agro-industrial society. Technological development and improvement of agronomical practices should lead to increase in production and reduction in the cost of production. This can be achieved by improved method of tillage; judicious and economic utilisation of land, water and inputs and adoption of suitable cropping patterns and other agronomical practices.

To rid agriculture in the tropical and sub-tropical areas of Kumaun Division from uncertainty, one of the necessary steps is to encourage the cultivation of drought-resistant crops and to popularise dry-farming methods in areas lacking in assured means of irrigation. Even good commercial crops, not necessarily food crops, as can thrive is scanty moisture should be recommended. The present yields of crops even under rainfed condition can be increased considerably with proper adoption of modern technology via proper agricultural extension and development of proper infra-structure and institutions. There is a great scope to develop vegetables and fruits and take advantage of regional production capability to develop inter-regional trade in vegetables and fruits further. The infrastructure needed for this purpose needs to be strengthened. Orchards could give the highest income per unit of hill land. With the present small scattered and fragmented holdings and lack of credit worthine˂s of farmers, the scope for orchards can be confined to larger farms.

Growing of fruits should also be an integral part of the development of economy of these villages in hill area. Almost every village in the hill provides scope for growing some fruits or the other. The potential is to be utilised to the full and once the programme is introduced in right earnest it has all the chances of success. We had a very pleasant experience, when once during the course of study tour, we came across a village in the Someshwar Valley of Almora District where all the eighty families and odd have their own kitchen gardens and small orchards, with the result that they were not only self-sufficient in seasonal fruits and vegetables, but were also exporting them in sizeable quantity to the neighbouring markets, and enjoying real prosperity through this unfalling source of supplementary income. On being questioned as to what further assistance they wanted from the department they replied that they wanted more and more technical know-how. Developing fruits and vegetable belts round focal points of hills will be a step forward in fortifying and strengthening the economy. This will ensure continuous supply of fruits and vegetables to places where there is heavy concentration of population and where local production to meet the requirement is not feasible. In fruit-belt areas a number of industries, e.g. processing industries, are sure to come up to boost the economy. If, however, production of fruits and vegetables is not taken up in compact areas the chances of the development of processing and allied industries remain remote. Lest there should be exploitation of vegetables and fruit growers, lest middle man should manipulate the market to their sole advantage, thus controlling and defeating the very purpose of horticultural development, public sector corporations or producer's cooperatives should be set up to handle the marketing.

Mandua, which is a very hardy and major crop but has poor yields owing to the need to keep field fellow could be replaced to a large extent by soyabeans, maize, vegetables, fruit plants and thus cropping intensity could be increased with suitable crop rotations. With the existing practice of slopes of more than 60 percent being put under the plough, soil erosion poses a great threat. If the potential for fruit development is fully utilised there would be one important advantage; and that is, fruit trees would provide a sort of semi-permanent vegetation which will correct ecological imbalance to a large extent.

No attempt to develop agriculture Horticulture in isolation will lead far. It is only with the creation of the socio-economic overheads that any economic progress can be sustained. An elaborate super-structure of technology and development must be supported on the framework of socio-economic overheads which form physical base.[3]

Roads play a crucial role in the development of the rural areas. Therefore, emphasis should be laid on the construction of a network of roads in the rural areas of Kumaun hills. Schemes of piped water supply and construction of diggis and naulas should be the other features of the rural development programmes in this area.

Rural industrialization has remained the weak link in the rural development programmes undertaken so far in Kumaun Division. Distribution of socio-economic overheads e.g., transport system, extension of civic amenities like, light and water, extension of social amenities, such as medical centres, community centres etc., should be a pre-condition to rural development. Rapid rural electrification programme also has a bearing on rural industrialization of Kumaun Division.

Community Involvement in I.R.D. Programme

The inevitable impact of P.R. bodies on the rural population is that they want a better living. Their association with the development efforts has increased the intensity of their desire. But their enthusiasm in individual projects of development is more than their desire to participate in the community works. They tend to depend upon Government grants instead of on voluntary contributions and upon Government efforts instead of on their personal participation.

The contributory factors to the slackening of people's participation are reduction in funds for the schemes, the compulsory element of matching contribution, lack of efforts on the part of leadership, appearance of group factions and divisive

3. *Community Development and Economic Development,* U.N. Study Report, Bangkok, 1968, p. 44.

trends, and lack of vitality in the panchayats of hill areas. People's contribution is an essential prerequisite for the success of efforts for economic reconstruction at a rapid pace in the context of resources of the Kumaun region. People's participation should be obtained in the form of sharing of expenditure on schemes by the village panchayat from its own resources.

In order to draw the people in all the activities of the panchayat before they are undertaken, it is necessary to convince them about the need and importance of such activities. Another step would be to formulate yearly programmes of projects to be undertaken on priority basis, which emerges from the felt need of the village people.

Local Planning

The Planning Commission emphasized the importance of local planning in order to make the Five-Year Plans realistic. It was obvious that the Panchayati Raj institutions were assigned a crucial role in the process of 'planning from below'. The process of local planning has a direct bearing on the functional aspect of the Panchayati Raj institutions. In order to make this institution meaningful, it is necessary to understand the nature of decision-making process as well as the nature of the decisions themselves.[4]

Although the principle of "planning from below" had been agreed long back, but in practice the plans are framed mostly at the State or Central level. This naturally resulted in the lack of enthusiasm at the local level in the execution of the various plan schemes. Even after 30 years of planning a number of local problems in hill areas still remain untouched. The benefits of development have not touched the down-trodden who are still living below the poverty line. In view of these lessons learnt from the earlier plans and to fully exploit the local resources, the present Government has taken the revolutionary decision of framing and executing plans at the district level with the active involvement of the people's representatives and the local officers.

The defect with out planning system is that its base is 'desk assumptions,' with little or no relation to any survey of actual local needs. Also, the decision-making process is schemewise, departmental and not integrative. The general tendency in the Secretariate is to build State plans in terms of prototype Central schemes—may be because of financial arrangements with the Centre with respect to the plan schemes. This had reduced planning into a mere distribution of financial resources from the state to the Parishads, Samitis and Village Panchayats.[5]

4. Nandedkar, V.G. : op. cit. p. 114.
5. *Report of the Agricultural Administration Committee*, New Delhi, Ministry of Food and Agriculture, Government of India, 1958, p. 45. "At present we have a *spectale* of financial targets being fulfilled without the proportionate additional production being realized."

In the thesis of planning from below the democratic institutions at the local level are not to be turned merely as a forum for obtaining the view of popular representatives but in due course should be capable of planning, the most suitable scheme that they consider beneficial to them. The Ford Foundation Team recommended that the programmes should be tailored to fit the local conditions 'village by village, block by block, area by area.'[6] The local representatives should be involved in the direction formulation and supervision of the schemes. The ultimate objective should be to develop the capacity at the local level to plan for themselves with given resources and those they can raise by themselves.

Integrated approach is another aspect of local planning. Development is a totality phenomenon and should find a balanced and simultaneous expression in all development activities conducted by various departments. The success of an irrigation tank depends equally on the successful planning of the use of water in the area it caters for, changes in the crop pattern of the area, extension of credit facilities, assured supply lines and secured marketing conditions. Even within the department itself the approach needs to be integrative. Thus, along with the expansion of the Primary Health Centres, provision of staff quarters, availability of competent M.B.B.S. doctors, adequate supply of medicines and effective health education, all need consideration. To an average village, the village Panchayat is an all-purposive organisation. His approach to development, therefore, is not piecemeal. So, the U.N. Report mentioned that a health service was only one aspect of planning at the local level. Many other services, like Agriculture, Education, are of equal importance. What is required is a balanced programme and not a heterogeneous series of unrelated movements.[7]

The main thrust of the local planning should be on execution of such schemes which yield quick results, with lesser investments, create avenues for employment and are productive in nature. The scheme suggested include Agriculture, Horticulture, Soil conservation, Minor Irrigation, Drainage Schemes, Dairy Development, Rural and Cottage Industries, Fisheries Department etc. It is expected that formulation of the scheme at the local level would identify the problems of the area and enlist co-operation of the people to solve them. It will also help in

6. *Report on India's Food Crisis and Steps to Meet it*, New Delhi, Ford Foundation Team, Ministry of Food and Agriculture and Ministry of Community Development and Co-operation, Government of India, 1959, p.18.
7. *W.H.O. Methodology of Planning : An Integrated Health Programme for Rural Areas*, II Report, Geneva, 1954, p. 44; *Decentralization for National and Local Development*, New York, Department of Economic and Social Affairs, U.N., 1962, p. 7; Ensiminger and Taylor, *India's Roots of Democracy*, op. cit., p. 173. Similar views were expressed by the Grow More Food Enquiry Committee, 1952, Government of India. "All aspects of rural life are inter-related and no lasting results can be achieved, if individual aspects of it are dealt with in isolation."

solving the problem of regional imbalance and help in optimum utilisation of local resources.

Co-ordination

No attempt to develop agriculture in isolation will lead far. A programme for educating the people to improve health and food habits, and for developing horticulture, animal husbandry, dairy industry, poultry and pisci-culture, should be included in the development plan for agriculture. To formulate and to promote such a composite plan the (subject matter) specialists concerned should work jointly. And, if agriculture is also to yield, raw material for industry, plan for agricultural development should be so drawn as to accommodate the requirements of feasible industries. An advance plan for suitable industrial development should be dove-tailed with the agricultural plan. There is perhaps no other way to regenerating the economy of Kumaun hills, except to have a well co-ordinated plan for the development of agriculture, horticulture, animal husbandry, industry, etc.

At present, the field services of non-pooled departments viz., the Sub-Deputy Inspectors of Schools, the Forest Panchayat Inspectors, the Range Officers or Foresters, the Kanungos, and the Patwaris have no real and direct relationship with the block staff and the Kshettra Samiti as regards the performance of the activities attached to their office. They deal directly with the village people and the subordinate staff of their respective departments in the field stations. They have to be guided by the instructions from their own departmental officers at the district level.

One of the obstacles in the effective implementation of I.R.D. programmes is the present day structure of C.D. blocks, enervated by dilution of powers and functions of the B.D.O. who is no longer looked upon as the effective leader and coordinator of block organization. Over the year, the departments have built up their respective lines of administration providing thereby direct administrative support for programme implementation. In the State like U.P. where the training and visit system of extension has been introduced, the village level workers have been put under the direct and exclusive charge of the Agriculture Department of district level and they are no longer available for implementation of block programmes. This kind of arrangements militate against the basic idea of integrating services at the lowest level of administrative hierarchy and cuts out at the root of block organisation. Thus, the powers and functions of the B.D.O. should be restored by placing him as the real executive officer in respect of all extension staff at the block level and nothing should be done to weaken the block structure, lest the implementational machinery be jeopardised. The block organisation should be strengthened in all possible ways so that it becomes an effective unit of planning and implementation. Unless the authority of B.D.O. over the block staff is restored and block structure revitalised, it will be difficult to formulate and implement I.R.D. plans. It may be suggested that the Block Development Officers should invariably be drawn from the cadre of State Civil Services, preferably of the rank of S.D.M. to make them more effective executive authority in matters of rural development.

It is necessary to bring the whole rural development programmes under one integrated authority. Such an authority will bring together all the elements of the programmes right from input supply to marketing of finished products including planning the extension advice. The confusion that sometimes arises between S.F.D.A and other rural development programme and the I.R.D. could thus be avoided if there is a unified agency to control and co-ordinate all the activities, since the objective of almost all the rural development programmes currently under implementation is the creation of increased employment and income, a unified agency at the district level would be able to provide better supervision and bring in a co-ordinated effort in the generation of employment opportunities. Co-ordination in the preparation of the plans should invariably follow co-ordination in implementation. The development programmes of panchayats and other development departments have to be co-ordinated at the village level. Hence the problem is not only of structural and organisational changes and alterations in procedure but also radical changes in the attitudes of public servants and the people's representatives and the promotion of decentralised, real self-governing popular institutions.

Finance

The problem of poor finance of panchayats has been an important factor which has hindered their proper and efficient functioning. Even the compulsory taxes and fees are not levied by most of the panchayats. Panchayats are empowered to levy various taxes and fees. But such direct taxation by the panchayats is resented by the people. Majority of the panchayats have failed to raise their annual income from their own local resources, to the extent of meeting the routine office expenditure consisting of stationery, forms, audit fee, and the like. Most of the panchayats in Kumaun have a very low income through which they cannot be expected to perform any civic activity.

The taxation powers given to the P.R. institutions should be more specific and must not operate iniquitously. Certain occupations and professions in which the weaker sections predominate should, however, be exempted through statutory provisions in order to ensure social justice.

Tax on land revenue can be replaced by a uniform system of assessing panchayat cess to be collected with land revenues and paid to the panchayats at the source. There exists no system of giving recurring government grants to the panchayats out of the general revenues or a certain percentage from a particular source of income, such as land revenues which could be utilized by the panchayats at their discretion for the performance of any activity imposed on them by the Act.

Without sufficient financial assistance from the State Government, the panchayats cannot continue their existence, because in these hill districts the scope for local taxation and other sources of income of the panchayats are very limited. In fact, in many cases even if the whole income from land revenues of the village were paid to its panchayat that would be quite inadequate. Hence the panchayats must be given government grants from the general revenues of the State Government. Side by side, more liberty should be given to the panchayats in making schemes for the utilization of money received by them as grants-in-aid. The chances of misappropriation may be checked through regular inspections, vigilance and guidance by the field staff, and through a system of regular audit.

Apart from the budgetary devolution from the State Government, the P.R. institutions should also be encouraged to mobilise enough resources of their own. No democratic institutions can continue to maintain its operational vitality by depending upon external resources only. The thesis "no taxation, only representation" should be discouraged. For this purpose, all P.R. institutions should have compulsory powers of taxation.[8] A select list of taxation powers should be given to the P.R. institutions and out of them some should be made compulsory. Certain taxes like house tax, profession tax, entertainment tax, special tax on land and buildings should be levied compulsorily by the P.R. institutions.

P.R. bodies have meagre resources of their own to fulfil their developmental functions. They have to depend on grants from the State Government for all developmental activities. To that extent, the effective control by local bodies over local development is affected and little scope is left for decision-making or administrative improvement at the local level. If this feeling develops, it would result in the progressive loss of interest in area planning and local development. "In the new context of development, establishment of a Panchayat Raj Finance Corporation and a Panchyati Raj Finance Commission would introduce much order in the present situation."[9]

To sum, up, for the I.R.D. it is necessary to lay adequate emphasis on collective effort, comprehensiveness of approach, economic realism and discipline,

8. Cf. The Committee on Panchayati Raj Institutions, op. cit.
9. Nandedkar, V.G. : op. cit. p. 185.

planned development of entrepreneurship and judicious allocation of resources.

Kumaun Division is still very much backward as compared to other districts of the State, because of its geographical situation, topographical condition, lack of means of communication, absence of irrigation facilities, lack of education, etc. In order to inject new ideas in the people concentrated and improved media of information and publicity needs to be pressed into action.

In the context of our experience of implementation of the existing I.R.D. programmes in this region, it can safely be stated that:

1. Promising approach to solving Kumaun's complex socio-economic rural problems with its depressing poverty, is through national policies in support of an integrated, area based, rural development programme. The present community development blocks should be accepted as the unit area for I.R.D. programmes.
2. Areas for development activities should be earmarked before activities start depending on the potential existing in an area for each activity. Implementation of various programmes are to be done by village panchayats, expert advice when needed should come from above.
3. In order to secure a more uniform rate of growth in the rural areas, a differentiated rate of investment should be made taking into account the relative backwardness in different parts of Kumaun Division.
4. It makes no difference whether the area being taken up for I.R.D. has assured water for irrigation or in a limited rain-fed area the development and modernization of horticulture and agriculture must be given top priority.
5. P.R. can be greatly strengthened and its role made more dynamic if the relationship between the panchayat as an institution of the people and the government staff at the district and block levels is clarified. The panchayats must see their role as being more dynamically developmental, and the governmental staff must view the panchayats as a means of getting the people to accept and do the things the village people's leaders and the government feel to be in the best interest of the people and the nation.[10]
6. Cooperative can play an important role in I.R.D. if they are well managed, function as people's institutions and operate under policies which make them competitive-operating without subsidies or having a monopoly over an area of service.
7. As important as the panchayats and co-operative institutions are, they cannot take the place of the more informal and many times more special interest orientation of voluntary organizations like farmers organization, women's organization, youth organization and children's organizations. These voluntary

10. Douglas Ensminger, *Rural India in Transition*, op. cit. p. 93.

organizations won't just come into being and function effectively without some outside initiative, guidance, leadership, training and assistance in sponsoring programmes which attract people's interest and meet the needs of village people. The V.L.W. and the B.D.O. can make a significant contribution to the development of these people's voluntary organizations and assist the organizations in understanding problems, weighing alternative solutions and taking appropriate action. "Rural development should be judged by the increase in quality of village leadership, social relations, institutions, voluntary organizations as they contribute to improving the quality of human life."

8. Since Kumaun Division is rich in forest resources, the forest resources can be utilized by village panchayat by opening cottage industries like making of furniture, wooden boxes, etc. It will also give employment to the unemployed rural folk who simply wander about for work from one place to another. Thus, this will enrich the economy of Kumaun.
9. Since financial resources of both Central and State Governments will never be adequate to do all the things needed in bringing parity of socio-economic services and communication facilities to Kumaun's thousand villages there are no alternatives to having the people join the government as partners in rural development—the government providing supplementary resources and technology and the people the leadership, institutions, motivations as well as resources of the people to do for themselves what they can do and look to government for encouragement, back-up support and know-how.[11] Given the nature and complexity of Kumaun's rural problems, the government and the people can have a meaningful partnership relation within a comprehensive integrated area development programme.
10. An I.R.D. programme will make possible planning, allocation of resources and implementation being a continuous process and, therefore, have more meaning and command greater support both from the people in the area and general public. This will assure planning from the bottom and action where the problems exist.
11. The effectiveness of an I.R.D. programme will be related to its boldness, Clarity of policies, leadership and response of village people, administrative machinery for coordination and implementation, quality of staff and how resources are allocated.
12. If an I.R.D. programme is to achieve its objective of contributing toward providing parity of socio-economic services and institutions and creating alternatives to agricultural employment opportunities in the Kumaun region, planners and political leaders must understand that the programme can

---

11. Douglas Ensminger, *Rural India in Transition*, op. cit. p. 94.

succeed only if backed by bold national policies; and by passing, implementing of essential legislation assuring equitable land holdings and tenure arrangements and providing needed finances.

13. Since a significant percentage of resources required to finance an I.R.D. programme will be Union funds, new approaches for making funds available to the states should be explored. The primary objective should be to find well planned and effectively executed programmes in ways that will contribute to strengthening local leadership and institutions.
14. Selection, training and supervision of the field staff for I.R.D. is of paramount importance. Since I.R.D. must be viewed as a process of change and growth, continuous inservice training will be essential and supervision which seeks to bring out the best of one's talents is imperative. People must be trained to do the jobs expected of them and helped through supervision to succeed in their assigned roles.
15. Given the importance of the district leadership, both official and non-official, in an I.R.D. programme and accepting the key role of the Zila Parishad in the district, it logically follows the Chief District Executive Officer should, at the district level, play the same role as the Development Commissioner at the State level, functioning under the overall guidance and direction of the Zila Parishad. He should be an officer of adequate seniority, highly competent, and dynamic. Since it is within the district that all rural development takes place, it is essential that the Chief District Executive Officer devotes his full time to co-ordinating all development programmes within the district and giving leadership to the functioning of all the different agencies of government and the Zila Parishad. He alone can assure an integrated approach to rural development in its entirety.
16. The V.L.W. holds the key that unlocks the minds and creates the conditions for village people to become concerned about problems and to examine alternative solutions. While the V.L.W. must know about alternative solutions, his job must be primarily one of creating village interest and desire to change, to improve and to try new things. He should know what the technical staff recommends in areas of agriculture, family planning and health and help the village people understand and apply technical recommendations.
17. Since the district, block and village staff giving leadership to I.R.D. must spend most of their time with the village people educating, encouraging, demonstrating and assisting in implementing plans and decisions taken, the kind and amount of reporting must be held to an absolute minimum. Too much emphasis on reporting achievements leads to falsifying accomplishments and makes paper workers out of staff. Those who should be working on the fields become desk-workers.

18. In integrated rural area development, people born in the villages can look forward to living and earning a living in the area of their birth and all can contribute towards culturally and economically enriching the area. Community Development and the Panchayati Raj institutions provide the framework for government and the people to work towards a common objective of providing the conditions in all the rural people of Kumaun Division.

P.R. institutions need not be looked upon narrowly as only an administrative construct to carry out development schemes. They have acted as modernizing agents in the rural life of Kumaun Division. In the words of Nichols Luyks, the P.R. institutions should "in developing structures appropriate to the process of modernization..." show "...more concern for the integration of rural governing institutions into a system of planning and implementation which joins the community to its external relationship."[12]

Endowed with adequate funds, vested with full executive authority and with development schemes in hand, P.R. institutions in these hill districts can enthuse the rural people to build a great potential modernizing force needed for I.R.D. programmes.

Faith and interest are the two sides of the same problem and have a direct bearing on the functional efficiency of the institution. These two would operate for the success of village panchayat and such a village panchayat would further the cause of Integrated Rural Development.

12. Quoted from Nandedkar, V.G. : op. cit. p. 188.

BIBLIOGRAPHY

Section one: Books

1. Akhter, H.K. : The Role of Women in a Country's Development, Commilla, PARD, July 1963.
2. Action for Rural Change : Readings in Indian Community Development, New Delhi, Oriental Publishers, 1970.
3. Agarwal, S.N. : Gandhian Constitution for Free India, Allahabad, Kitabistan, 1946.
4. Arthur, F. Raper : Rural Development in Action, Ithaca and London, Cornell University Press, 1970.
5. Atkinson, E.T. : Statistical, Descriptive and Historical Account of the North-Western Provinces of India, Vol. IV, Allahabad, North-Western Provinces Government Press, 1946.
6. Arora, R.C. : Integrated Rural Development, New Delhi, S. Chand and Company Ltd., 1979.
7. Batten, T.R. : Training for Community Development, London, Oxford University Press, 1973.
8. Bayard, H.P. (Edited) : Rural Reconstruction and Development, New Yord, Frederick A. Praeger, Publishers, 1967.
9. Bhargava, B.S. : Emerging Leadership in Panchayati Raj System, Bangalore, Institute of Social and Economic Change, 1977.
10. Bhargava, B.S. : Grass Roots Leadership, New Delhi, Ashish Publishing House, 1979.
11. Betille, A. : Caste, Class and Power, Changing Patterns of Stratification in a Tanjore Village, Bombay, Oxford University Press, 1966.
12. Bhattacharya, S.N. : Community Development, Calcutta - 9, Academic Publishers, 1970.
13. Burton, W.K., Aiton, E.W., Andrew, P.T. : Leadership for Action in Rural Communities, INC. Danville, Illinois, U.S.A., The Interstate Printers and Publishers, 1965.
14. Chandra, H. : Problems and Prospects of Road Transport Development in Hill Areas of U.P. with special reference to Kumaun Region, Ph.D. Dissertation, Nainital, Kumaun University, 1976.
15. Case Studies in Panchayati Raj : Committee on Case Studies, IIPA, New Delhi, Indraprastha Estate, 1972.
16. Dey, S.K. : Community Development, New York, Asia Publishing House, 1962.
17. Deshmukh, C.D. : Aspects of Development, New Delhi, Young Asia Publication, 1972.
18. Deshmukh, Durgabai. (Edited) : Social Welfare in India, Howrah, Glasgow Printing Co., Ltd., 1955.

19. Ensminger Douglas : Rural India in Transition, New Delhi, Thomson Press (India) Limited, 1972.
20. Frey, F.W. : The Turkish Political Elite, Cambridge, M.I.T. Press, 1965.
21. Gaikwad, V.R. : Panchayati Raj and Bureaucracy, A Study of the Relationship Patterns, Hyderabad, National Institute of Community Development, 1969.
22. Gandhi, M.K. : Rebuilding Our Villages.
23. Geoffery, D. : The Organisation and Practice of Local Government, London, Melbourne, Toronto, William Heinemann Ltd., 1969.
24. Haq, M.S. : Community Development Through Extension, Allahabad, Chugh Publications, 1979.
25. Hanson, A.H. : The Process of Planning, A study of India's Five Year Plans 1950 - 1964, Bombay, Oxford University Press, 1966.
26. Inamdar, N.R. : Functions of Village Panchayats in Jeorge Jacob (Ed.) Readings on Panchayati Raj, Hyderabad, N.I.C.D., 196.
27. Jain, S.C. : Community Development and Panchayati Raj in India, Bombay, Allied Publishers, 1967.
28. Jha, S.N. : Leadership and Local Politics, Bombay, Popular Prakashan Private Ltd., 1979.
29. Kavoori, J.C. and Singh, B.N. : History of Rural Development in Modern India, Vol. I, New Delhi, Impex India, 1967.
30. Khushalani, K.B. : Irrigation (Practise and Design) Vol. I and II, Poona, Allied Book Stall, 1962.
31. Kotter, H.R. : Some Observation on Basic Principles and General Strategy Under Statics, Vol. 12, No. 4, 1974.
32. Krishnaswami, K.S. : Some Thoughts on A Drama, Finance and Development, Washington, I.M.F., Vol. I, 1969.
33. Khan, Waheeduddin., Tripathy, R.N. : Plan for Integrated Rural Development in Pauri Garhwal, Hyderabad, National Institute of Community Development, Avon Printing Press, 1976.
34. Khan, Iltiza. : Government in Rural India, Bombay, Asia Publishing House, 1969.
35. Kreitton, Aiton, and Torrence. : Leadership for Action in Rural Communities, Inc. Danville, Illinois, The Interstate Printers and Publishers, 1965.
36. Kavoori, J.C. Baij Nath Singh : History of Rural Development in Modern India, New Delhi, Impex India, 1967.
37. Lokanathan, V. : Essays in Indian Economic Development, New Delhi, S. Chand and Company Ltd., 1979.
38. Sen, Lalit K. : Abdul, L. Thalia. : Regional Planning for a Hill Area, N.I.C.D., Hyderabad, Swarajya Printing Institute, Secunderabad, 1976.
39. Madan, G.R. : Changing Pattern of Indian Villages, New Delhi, S. Chand and Company., 1964.
40. Malenbanum, W. : Prospects for Indian Development, London, George Allen and Unwin Ltd., 1962.
41. Maddick, Henry. : Panchayati Raj - A Study of Rural Local Government in India, London, Longman Group Ltd., 1970.

42. Malviya, H.D. : Village Panchayats in India, New Delhi, All India Congress Committee, 1956.
43. Mathur, M.V. and Others : Panchayat Raj in Rajasthan, New Delhi, Impex India, 1966.
44. Mehta, S.R. : Emerging Pattern of Rural Leadership, New Delhi, Wiley Eastern Private Limited, 1972.
45. Misra S.N. : Pattern of Emerging Leadership in Rural India, Patna, Associated Book Agency, 1977.
46. Misra, R.P., Sundaram, K.V. : Rural Area Development Perspectives and Approach, New Delhi, Sterling Publishers Pvt. Ltd., 1978.
47. Meier, Richard L. : Development Planning, New York, McGraw Hill Book Company, 1965.
48. Mukherjee, Ramkrishna. : Six Villages of Bengal, Bombay, Popular Prakashan, 1971.
49. Mukherji, B. : Community Development in India, New Delhi, Orient Longmans Limited, 1967.
50. Naithani, R.C. : Water Resources of Kumaun, Unpublished Doctoral Dissertation, Agra, Agra University, 1972.
51. N.C.A.E.R. : Rehabilitation and Development of Basti District, Delhi, Asia Publishing House, 1959.
52. N.C.A.E.R. : Techno-Economic Survey of U.P., N.C.A.E.R., Delhi, 1965.
53. Narain, I. and Others : Rural Elite and Elections in an Indian State, National Publishing house, 1976.
54. Narain, I., Pande, K.C., Sharma, M.L. : The Rural Elite in an Indian State, New Delhi, Manohar Book Service, 1976.
55. Narain, J.P. : Communitarian Society and Panchayati Raj, Village in Free India, Varanasi, Navachetna Prakashan, 1970.
56. Narain, J.P. : Socialism, Sarvodaya and Democracy, New York, Asian Publishing House, 1964.
57. Otto, G. Hoiberg. : Exploring the Small Community, Lincoln, University of Nebraska Press, 1955.
58. Pant, S.D. : Social Economy of the Himalayas, London, George Allen and Unwin Ltd., 1935.
59. Pandey, P.C. : A Study of Changes in Economic Conditions of Scheduled Caste in Kumaun Since Independence, unpublished Ph.D. Thesis from Agra University, 1978.
60. Paddiel, H. : Panchayati Raj, A Study of Rural Local Government in India, Longmans, 1970.
61. Papola, T.S. and Others : Studies on Development of Uttar Pradesh, Lucknow, Saha Works, 1979.
62. Panchanadikar, K.C., Panchanadikar, J. : Rural Modernization in India, Bombay, Popular Prakashan, 1978.
63. Park, C., Richard, Tinker, I. : Leadership and Political Institutions in India (edited), Oxford University Press, 1960.
64. Planning Research and Action Institute, U.P. : Communication and Leadership in Bajpokhar Gram Sabha. (A Case Study of Panchayat Election).

65. Planning Research and Action Institute : Factionalism and Leadership Change in Phurbharal. (A Case Study of Panchayat Election), Lucknow, March, 1964.
66. Raper, F. Arthur; Rural Development in Action, Ithaca and London, Cornell University Press, 1970.
67. Samual, P.H. : Political Order in Changing Societies, New Haven, Yale University Press, 1970.
68. Sharib, Z.H. : Problems of Rural Reconstruction in India, (with special reference to V. I), Bombay, The All India Institute of Local Self-Government, 1958.
69. Sharma, M.P. : Evolution of Rural Local Self-Government in U.P., All India Institute of Local Self-Government, Bombay, 1957.
70. Sharma, S.K. and Malhotra, S.L. : Integrated Rural Development Approach Strategy and Perspectives, New Delhi, Abinav Publication, 1977.
71 Sen, K. Lalit, Thaha, L. Abdul, Regional Planning for a Hill Area, Hyderabad, National Institute of Community Development, Secunderabad, Swarajya Printing Institute, 1976.
72. Selzmick, Philip. : Leadership in Administration, New York, Harper and Row; INC., Tokyo, John Weatherhill, 1966.
73. Sharma, Sudesh Kumar. : Dynamics of Development, Delhi Concept Publishing Company, 1977.
74. Shah, S.M. : Rural Development Planning and Reforms, New Delhi, Abinav Publication, 1977.
75. Sharma, M.P. : Local Self-Government and Finance in U.P., Allahabad, Kitab Mahal, 1954.
76. Singh, Avtar. : Leadership Pattern and Village Structure; A Study of Six Indian Villages, New Delhi, Sterling Publishers, 1973.
77. Singh, Harjinder.; Village Leadership (A Case Study of Village Mohali in Punjab), Delhi, Sterling Publishers, 1968.
78. Sirsikar, V.M. : The Ruling Elite in a Developing Society, A Study in Political Sociology, Orient Longmans, Ltd., 1970.
79. Talyer, G.C. Douglas, E., Helen, W.J., Jean, J. : India's Roots of Democracy, New Delhi, Orient Longmans Limited, 1965.
80. Tewari, G.D. : Rural Self Government in Kumaun Hills, Agra University Ph.D. Thesis (Unpublished), 1962.
81. Tondon, B.C. : Economic Planning : Principles and Problems, Allahabad, Chaitanya Publishing House, 1963.
82. Upholf, N. and Esman, N. : Local Organisation for Rural Development, Analysis of Asian Experience, Ithaca, Cornell University Press, 1972.
83. Venktarangia, M., Pattabhiram, M. : Local Government in India (Select Reading), Bombay, Allied Publishers Private Limited, 1969.
84. Waterston, Albert. : Development Planning Lessons of Experience, Baltimore Marryland, The John Hopkins Press, 1969.

Section Two: Original Sources

1. Report of the Committee on Panchayati Raj Institutions, Government of India, Ministry of Agriculture and Irrigation, Department of Rural Development, August 1978, New Delhi.
2. Report of the Study Team on Panchayati Raj, Panchayat and Development Department, Government of Rajasthan, 1964.
3. Report of the Committee for Evaluation and on Public Participation, Uttar Pradesh, 1959.
4. Report of the Committee on Democratic Decentralisation, Co-operation and Rural Development Department, Government of Maharashtra, 1962.
5. The Report of the Study Team on Panchayati Raj Finance, Ministry of Community Development and Co-operation, Government of India, New Delhi, 1963.
6. Report of the Local Finance Enquiry Committee, National Government, 1950.
7. Report of the Team for the Study of Community Projects and National Extension Service, Committee on Plan Projects, New Delhi, 1957.
8. Indian Government Second Five Year Plan, Planning Commission, 1956.
9. Agricultural Census 1970-1971, U.P.
10. Report of Congress Village Panchayat Committee, 1954, All India Congress Committee Office, New Delhi, p. 16.
11. Report of the U.P. Evaluation Committee, 1959.
12. U.P. Panchayati Raj Act, 1947.
13. Kshettra Samitis and Zila Parishad Adhiniyam.
14. Guidelines for Intensive Development of Blocks under the Programme for I.R.D., Vol. II (Annexes), New Delhi, Ministry of Agriculture and Irrigation, Government of India, 1978.
15. Rural Development Programme in India, New Delhi, Ministry of Agriculture and Irrigation, Government of India, 1978.
16. Report of the U.P. Panchayat Raj Amendment Act Committee, 1954, Lucknow, Supdt: Printing and Stationery, U.P., 1954.
17. Project Report, Hill Area Development Agency, Pithoragarh, 1977-78, 1981-82 (U.P.)
18. Government of India : The First Five-Year Plan, Planning Commission, Delhi, 1952.
19. U.P., Industries Reorganisation Committee Report (1934).
20. Emerging Patterns of Rural Leadership in Southern Asia (Report on an International Round Table Conference), Government of India, N.I.C.D., Hyderabad, 1965.
21. Evaluation Report on Working of C.D. and N.E.S. Blocks, April, 1957.
22. Report of the Fourth National Conference, Panchayati Raj Perspective and Programme, New Delhi, A.I.P.P., 1964.
23. Report of the Committee on Panchayati Raj Finance, New Delhi, Government of India, Ministry of Community Development, 1963.

24. The Report of the Committee on Panchayati Raj Finances, Government of Mysore, Bangalore, 1963.
25. Report of the Evaluation Committee on Panchayati Raj, Bombay, Government of Maharashtra, 1971.

Section Three: Journal

1. The Indian Journal of Public Administration, Indian Institute of Public Administration, New Delhi.
2. Quarterly Journal of the Local Self-Government Institute (Bombay). The All India Institute of Local Self-Government.
3. Indian Journal of Political Science, Quarterly of the Indian Political Science Association, Chandigarh.
4. The Civic Affairs, A Monthly Journal of City Government in India, Kanpur.
5. Krukshetra, Fortnightly Journal of Community Development and Village Democracy.
6. Economic Weekly.
7. Urban and Rural Planning Thought, School of Planning and Architecture, New Delhi.
8. Rural Development Digest, National Institute of Rural Development, Hyderabad.
9. Social Action.
10. Social Welfare, New Delhi, C.S.W.B.

Section Four: Miscellaneous (Field Studies and Research Papers)

1. Resource Inventory and Integrated Rural Development Plan for Tehri Garhwal District (Project Report). G.B. Pant University of Agriculture and Technology, Nainital, 1976.
2. Integrated Rural Development Plan for Bhimtal Block in Nainital District. G.B. Pant University of Agriculture and Technology, Nainital, 1976.
3. Regional Seminar on Planning for Integrated Rural Area Development, Sponsored by the Ministry of Education and Social Welfare, Department of Education, G.B. Pant University of Agriculture and Technology, Nainital, 1977.
4. Norman Reynolds, Local Level Rural Institutions, Agenda Paper for the Session with Messers Staples and Shaw, Singapore.
5. A.P. Singh. Local Government and Integrated Rural Development. Almora District: A Case Study, Indian Institute of Management, Ahmedabad, 1974.
6. Economic Times.
7. Inauguration of the Panchayat Bhawan, Jotwar, Rajasthan, Jaipur, 13th Nov., 1955.

Index

Q

R

S

T

U

V

W

Y

Z